Struggling with Forgiveness

*is a Path Book
offering practical spirituality
to enrich everyday living.*

*"Your word is a lamp to my feet
and a light to my path."*
Psalm 119:105

Struggling with Forgiveness

Stories from People and Communities

David Self

Path Books
A LIGHT TO MY PATH

Path Books

an imprint of ABC Publishing

Anglican Book Centre

600 Jarvis Street

Toronto, Ontario

Canada M4Y 2J6

Marian Partington's story has been adapted and reprinted from Alistair McFadyen and Marcel Sarot, eds., *Forgiveness and Truth: Explorations in Contemporary Theology* (Edinburgh: T&T Clark). Used with permission.

The three stories in the section, "Healing among Aboriginal Peoples in Canada," were transcribed with grateful acknowledgement from the video, *The Healing Circle,* produced by Anglican Video, 1995.

National Library of Canada Cataloguing in Publication

Self, David
        Struggling with forgiveness : stories from people and communities / David Self.
ISBN 1-55126-395-5
1.Forgiveness—Religious aspects—Christianity. I.Title.

BV4647.F55S44 2003   234'.5   C2003-902453-9

Printed in Canada

Contents

Preface

When my bishop suggested I take three months away for a sabbatical, I was surprised. I wondered what I would do with the time. As I pondered, the word "forgiveness" kept coming up, and I realized that I wasn't sure what it really meant.

I had grown up thinking that forgiveness was something that happened quickly. You did something wrong, said you were sorry, and they forgave you. Or else someone hurt you, and you forgave them. That was it — and then everything carried on as if the hurt had never happened. But life in the real world isn't like this. I found that I was remembering painful incidents of twenty years earlier with great anger, and I discovered that I hadn't forgiven people at all. It wasn't easy to let go the anger and come to rest over the memories. A betrayal of trust is difficult to get over, especially if the hurt runs deep. In my view, such betrayal is sinful — it can lead to the wounding, or even the breaking up, of a relationship.

Listening to people over thirty years of ministry has taught me that forgiveness is both complicated and costly. So it occurred to me that I might go and ask others about their experience of forgiving, being forgiven, or not being able to give or receive forgiveness. And this is what happened. Everywhere I went, people were clear that "forgiveness" was a word with meaning for them, but they did not attempt to define it. Instead, they would tell me a story from their own lives. It was a humbling experience to be allowed to enter such holy ground — the hearts of those who were willing to trust me with their memories.

When we want to get to know each other, we share stories from our lives, entrusting them with a sense of risk. Stories have a richness of texture, a depth of meaning, a uniqueness of character. They may be told through words, gestures, ritual, art, music, or dance, but stories that come from the heart can touch other hearts. With great courage people shared something of their lives with me, and out came their treasures from within. Of course, the stories emerged through the filter of personal understanding and memory. Others might have interpreted or remembered the same incidents differently, because their perspectives, values, and assumptions were different. But all the people I met struggled to be as honest as possible with themselves. The result was a treasury of stories so powerful that I felt I had to share some of them to encourage others in their own life journeys.

My selection of stories attempts to reflect the tremendous range of human experience engaging with forgiveness: conflict in families or at work, conflict between individuals or within whole societies — murder, communal strife, colonial oppression, terrorist violence. There are struggles to forgive another, to be forgiven, to forgive oneself. There are struggles to live within emotional paralysis, struggles to persist in faith and courage, as people tried to be honest, human, and creative in costly ways. The stories are powerful. I have chosen them not because they define the only circumstances in which forgiveness can operate, but because they illustrate the processes we all go through, even when the events in our own lives seem less significant than those in the stories. There is much more to forgiveness than I had realized — such pain, such possibility for release and healing, such richness— and it is worth knowing that we are not alone in the struggle to make sense of our lives.

It might be helpful to distinguish among forgiveness, trust, and reconciliation. In my view, forgiveness is the healing process by which we try to deal with the pain of betrayal and the moral responsibility involved. But forgiveness does not automatically lead to a rebuilding of trust. I might employ someone released from prison, but I would not readily place an accountant convicted of fraud in charge of my accounts. Some trust may be rebuilt, but not all. And reconciliation? I may be forgiven by someone I have hurt, but we will not necessarily be reconciled. Reconciliation — that is, the restoration of relationship — needs a new formation of trust. Indeed, "restoration" may be the wrong word, because the experience has changed us both, and any future relationship will be different from the past. If we can recognize and accept the frailties within each of us, the relationship may continue and deepen. Or it may not.

It might also be helpful to say what I believe forgiveness is not. Forgiveness is not a condoning of the offence. It is not pretending that "it doesn't matter." Such an attitude tends to trivialize the event, deny the wound, avoid the cost, obscure any evil. This approach compounds the hurt with a lie, denying justice and personal responsibility, thereby blocking any creative ways of growing through the past.

Forgiveness is much more than just the absolution of guilt. It is a creative response that seeks a release from the hurt inflicted.

The offering of forgiveness is not conditional upon repentance. If the perpetrator is unknown or dies or refuses to admit responsibility, the victim is not necessarily locked in paralysis, unable to move through the hurt of betrayal. The struggle to come to an attitude of forgiveness takes place within the victim. On the other hand, the receiving of forgiveness does depend upon repentance. If the perpetrator acknowledges the offence, admits moral responsibility, and truly desires to change, he or she becomes open to receiving forgiveness. But repentance cannot demand forgiveness. If I have wronged someone, and I turn to them admitting my fault, I can only seek forgiveness in vulnerability; I cannot demand it.

Can forgiveness be a creative way of breaking the destructive cycles of rage, revenge, violence, or bitterness — for communities as well as individuals? I have glimpsed the appalling cost so many millions of people all over the world have carried in the twentieth century through warfare, civil strife, and communal conflict. I cannot really imagine what it is like to live and raise a family in the middle of brutal violence found in places such as Sarajevo, the Middle East, Sudan, Chechnya, much of Latin America, Cambodia, Kosovo, Sierra Leone … the list could go on and on.

Forgiveness is a real word in individual lives and families. But can it be applied to communities? Is it possible for communities to forgive each other as they emerge from a particular conflict? Can they learn to move beyond past hurts and fears, and if so, how? So I went to Belfast in Northern Ireland and to Cape Town in South Africa. My editor, Greig Dunn, inquired in Canada. These are three regions among the many troubled spots in the world where people are struggling with pain-filled histories and attitudes that have entrapped them in violence and abuse in the past. What healing is possible? We are not just isolated individuals; we are part of communities too. Communal attitudes and events affect us all, just as our personal actions and attitudes affect others.

The beginning of a new millennium seemed a good time to be asking such questions. Outside our church we planted a millennium yew tree, an act of hope for the future. It is a small sprig about six inches high, grown from the seed of a yew tree that was alive when Jesus was born some two thousand years ago. Yew trees can live an incredibly long time, and there are a few that, I am told, may have lasted five thousand years. They grow very slowly according to the conditions of weather, soil, and sun. Like all trees, they carry the marks and scars of the years and, as they grow older, those scars become part of their beauty. A good picture of human lives growing in forgiveness!

In our outer lives we have come to expect rapid growth influenced by instant communication, quick responses, "fix-it-now." But our inner lives grow much more slowly. Working through the scars of betrayal, for example, takes a long time. Every story in this book covers many years, and even now each person continues to struggle with forgiveness. Communal attitudes and social behaviour change still more slowly. The histories of communal conflict in Northern Ireland and South Africa stretch over centuries. So does the experience of oppression among Indigenous Peoples in Canada. The courage, the struggle to grow creatively, the sustained hope that is a fruit of endurance, were wonderful to encounter.

And so I share some of their stories (with the permission of those who told them to me) in the hope that their struggles may encourage others to keep on exploring, with God's help, the possibilities of forgiveness. I did not assume anything about people's faith. Many of them brought it into their narrative naturally, drawing strength from their own experience of God.

I believe in a God who is constantly at work in his world, creating, healing, transforming — a God who loves this creation far more deeply than we can ever imagine, but whose love can be glimpsed in the ministry of Jesus on earth. This belief led me to ask how such stories deepen our understanding of the forgiveness lying at the heart of the Christian gospel. How do Christ's life, passion, death, and resurrection help us to see more clearly what it means to say that God forgives us? I try to address these questions briefly at the end of the book.

This book does not have to be read from beginning to end. You can move through it, browsing here and there, to find points of connection. Many chapters touch on family experiences, some on early trauma, others on living within deeply divided communities. Sometimes forgiveness is possible; sometimes it seems impossible. Reading someone else's story can give you space to absorb it at your own pace, allowing it to interact with your own experiences, drawing out insights that the storyteller may not have thought of.

There are many ways to approach a story. For example, you might imagine that you are listening to the person sitting in front of you and then ask yourself, What feelings emerge for me? What insights? Would I share my story with them? If so, what would I say? If not, what prevents me?

I offer this book with gratitude to those who so willingly gave of themselves. Only a selection of the stories has been included, but I honour all those who shared with me something of their lives. Some names have been changed and the context altered, where necessary, to protect privacy. Marion graciously gave permission for her name to be used, as did those in Northern Ireland, South Africa, and Canada.

Since I have been living outside Canada for so long, I do not feel close enough to events there to comment on them, but the situation of Indigenous Peoples in Canada raises many issues pertinent to forgiveness. I am grateful to Robert Maclennan for providing stories collected by his colleague, Lisa Barry, senior producer of Anglican Video, who produced a video on the subject. Greig Dunn wrote the introduction and commentary, with the assistance of both Donna Bomberry, Native Affairs Coordinator, and Esther Wesley, Indigenous Healing Fund Coordinator, for the General Synod of the Anglican Church of Canada.

Collecting the stories in Northern Ireland and South Africa would not have been possible without the generosity of funders who were intrigued by the proposal, and of the staff and congregation of my parish, who readily gave me the time to do it. Robert Maclennan my publisher, and Greig Dunn, my editor, with whom I have been friends for longer than we care to admit, gave me invaluable guidance. Judith Cafelas undertook the laborious task of transcribing the spoken text onto the page. Nothing would have emerged without the persistent encouragement of many others in my own life, including Christopher Richards, John Townroe, Mary Ann Coates, Ann Bowes, Mike and Tess Featherstone, Sr. Annaliese, CSC, and members of my parish. I thank them all. And it would not have been possible at all without the sustained support of my wife, Carole, with whom I have learned so much about life and loving for many years.

Personal Forgiveness

Hurt and Healing

Enfolding the Dark

Marian's Story

On 24 February 1994 the police came to 25 Cromwell Street, Gloucester, in England to search for the body of Heather West by digging in the back garden. Heather had disappeared at the age of sixteen in 1987. The police found not only her body but many other bodies that had been buried in the garden and in the basement of the house. Heather's parents, Frederick and Rosemary West, were charged with abducting, torturing, raping, and killing an unknown number of girls and women over a period of twenty years. Frederick, who had previously been convicted of child abuse, was arrested and confessed to some of the killings, telling the police where they could find the bodies. He committed suicide while in custody. Rosemary was also arrested and convicted on ten counts of murder on 22 November 1995. She is now serving a life sentence.

Lucy Partington, my sister, "disappeared" in December 1973. In March 1994 we learned that she was one of the young women murdered by Frederick and Rosemary West. I found those twenty years increasingly difficult, not knowing what had happened to her. I felt anxious because you can't know what is going to happen from one moment to the next, and sometimes people even disappear; and this contributed to my becoming quite self-destructive. I couldn't trust life, and I made decisions that made my life very difficult and hurt other people at times.

People would say things that made me really angry, like, "God chooses the best and takes them young." For two decades of my life there was huge confusion because nothing was resolved, and it became almost taboo in the family to talk about Lucy. We hadn't had the ritual of a funeral, everything was on hold, and it was as if part of me was frozen.

We always tried to get together on Lucy's birthday, though even then we wouldn't talk about her much. It was almost as if we could avoid facing the probability that she had been murdered if we didn't talk about her. I couldn't face it until about three years before we found out.

In December 1993 I suggested that we plant a tree in memory of her, and we all got together. My daughter, who is incredibly honest and direct, commented afterwards that none of us mentioned her name, and she realized at that moment how painful it was and how stuck we all were.

Three months later they started digging up the bodies. We phoned the police and asked if their digging had anything to do with Lucy. At that point they had dug up only three bodies, but they said they would let us know. Later they revealed there were five more and one of them was called Lucy. When I received this news, I was very grateful to be in a stable, loving relationship.

The Quakerism and the Ch'an Buddhism that I explore have in common the medium of silence. Part of my personal theology relates to a dream that I had shortly after Lucy disappeared.

In the dream Lucy came back, and I said, "Where have you been?" She said, "I have been sitting in a water meadow near Grantham. If you sit very still, you can hear the sun move." The dream seemed to convey profound inner peace, and it reminded me of the words, "Be still and know that I am God."

I woke up with the sense that the dream was a real communication telling me that, whether Lucy was dead or alive, she was all right. Part of me really wants to know how to get back to that state of feeling the peace that passes all understanding, because when you are in it, everything seems to work and forgiveness is a spontaneous, authentic, permanent act. However, I know that it is very difficult to get there, and that forgiveness is not easily done.

All our rituals of laying to rest were healing acts. Several weeks after Lucy's bones were removed from Cromwell Street, I had a dream about embracing a skeleton that then became Lucy, and she put her head on my shoulder. I woke up feeling that I had to physically honour her. I had to wrap the bones and treat them with love and respect, because we didn't know how long they would have to stay in the mortuary during the trial. The whole ritual was profoundly healing.

Later we were able to have a requiem mass for Lucy with the dear priest who had prepared her to be received into the Roman Catholic Church five weeks before she was murdered. He had been praying for her every day since she disappeared. We were able to rebury her with reverence and love in a place that was important to her — the little twelfth-century church next to Hailes Abbey, where there are medieval wall paintings that Lucy had been studying. Later we had the gravestone setting ceremony. All these rituals were helpful and necessary, although one of my children said, "Oh no, not another thing. When are we going to stop?" But it was important that they be involved too because they were learning a process of grieving.

I made a vow at the end of one of my Buddhist retreats — I think it was in 1998 — to try to forgive the people who killed Lucy, and immediately afterward, when I got home, I felt extremely violent rage. It was a huge eruption, beyond logic or words, which was terrifying. At that moment I knew that I was capable of killing, and recognizing that connected me immediately to the Wests. Then I knew that part of the process of forgiveness was facing within myself my own potential for perpetrating abuse or being a victim.

I have been learning that forgiveness is a long process, and that it's rather pretentious and hypocritical of me to think that I can forgive the Wests before I have actually faced up to people in my own life whom I need to be forgiven by and whom I would like to forgive. In a way I am left with trying to stay true to what is actually happening and avoid nothing. That's where the teaching is, I think. I know that I can't find God in the Wests until I find God in myself. But finding God in myself involves facing my own potential for evil and destructive acts.

I am trying to understand and experience the profound reality of who I am, knowing that I am sacred and all life is sacred. I would like Rosemary West to know something of that. I have had a dream about trying to forgive her that revealed I wasn't ready to do it. But I think I'm getting closer. I'm trying to find a voice for the light without denying the reality of the darkness, and to explore the relationship between the two. That's where the crucifixion and the resurrection come in. In the process of exploring I have to be true to the fact that the light does seem to go out sometimes. I saw a lovely poster of a candle stating that it's better to strengthen the light than rail against the darkness. That's what my journey is about: finding ways to strengthen the light, so that whatever happens now will not destroy me too.

The image I had in my dream of Rosemary West was of utter darkness. The first scene was of meeting her and my saying, "I forgive you" — and it was meaningless! In the second scene she was sitting in a basement beside a pile of flesh, and putting handfuls of flesh into little polyethylene bags and throwing them out a hole in the wall, saying, "I keep throwing them away, but the sea keeps bringing them back." When she looked at me, I don't think she could see me. Her eyes looked like two sharp points trying to push themselves out of a black bin liner. It was as if something awful was going to burst out, and it was terrifying.

I sometimes use that dream almost like the Ignatian practice of meditation. I go back into it and realize that the monstrous image of the eyes is me. That sort of darkness is within me. This dream came up within me; it's part of my unconscious. I come back to the words of the dream and realize that you can't just throw things away. The sea will bring them back. Perhaps if I sit with that image I can help Rosemary West understand this meaning.

I'm learning how to forgive myself, and I'm learning to believe that others can forgive me. In this process I've explored my own rotting pile of mistakes, but I also see that it's my compost. It has a meaning. It doesn't have to remain repulsive, something I can't acknowledge, something I want to edit out. It actually is part of who I am, and I have to develop another relationship with it. Once I have really accepted all this, I'll know that I don't have to make those mistakes again. I'll know who I am, that my life is sacred, that we do have real choices, and that every moment is an opportunity to go forward toward the light. What happened to Lucy makes it urgent for me to find what could possibly give us strength to transcend the human capacity for atrocity.

A thing that especially horrifies me is that she was gagged so that she couldn't speak her truth. The minute she was gagged she became mere flesh and bones. She had already lost who she was. She loved words and the beauty of life with refined sensibility, and she wanted to go on and study literature. It's very painful to think of her tied up in a basement with people who were her total opposites. That's why it's important for me to find my truth and speak it, including the truth that died with Lucy.

I feel that I'm most true to myself when I'm vulnerable and open to pain. Creativity comes when you have accepted, faced, and experienced the pain. Only then are you free to forgive. When the pain is still unacknowledged or in control, anything you do has the potential to carry negative emotions that destroy. Hatred, anger, rage, vengeance, all come from that place of pain. I think the actions of the Wests come from that place. So I have compassion for them because I know that once you are brutalized, you lose the sense of who you are, the sense of beauty, the sense that God is within you.

Learning How
to Remember

Joy's Story

I had been teaching for twenty-seven years, and the last few were incredibly hard because I found it very difficult to administer the kind of discipline that was required in the school where I worked. Being a fairly senior member of staff, I was expected to be able to get everything right and to deal effectively with awkward children. The school was known to be difficult, and to complicate matters there were lots of problems at the management level. I had supported the headmistress in her struggles, which made it all the more difficult when she decided not to support me. The crunch came just before Easter one year when she told me I had to get my act together. She didn't tell me that this was a formal verbal warning, so I was surprised when I received a letter that began, "Because of your continued failure to do your work as senior mistress in the school, I am going to put you on a disciplinary procedure."

I had already decided that I couldn't survive much longer in that school and had made an appointment to talk to somebody about taking early retirement. It was probably a week before I read beyond the first sentence of the letter, because I had put a lot into my work and I thought the headmistress was a friend. I was really very angry and humiliated. I think the anger was my salvation because it made me absolutely determined that I wasn't going to let this destroy me. The actual procedure about early retirement took its course. I was off school for the whole summer term, and at the beginning of the summer holiday the news came that I was going to be allowed to retire.

This took place twelve years ago, and it still hurts. I felt as though I had been dismantled — I think that's the way to describe it. I found that there was a great struggle between the anger I felt about the way I had been treated and the requirement I felt to forgive the person who had done it. She didn't seem to think anything untoward had happened. When she learned that I had got the offer of a job outside teaching, she said, "Ah well, there you are, you see. It will all be all right." It seemed as if she was saying that getting me out of the school was good for me! I wasn't going to let her get away with that. She had been cruel, and there were ways of dealing with the situation that would have been more creative all round.

When it was official that I was leaving, the staff wanted to give me a leaving present. I said, "Yeah, okay. I'll come and say goodbye and receive the gift, but I want to talk to the head first." I told her that I would come and be given a fond farewell from those who wished to do it, but that I didn't want her to think what had happened didn't matter. It was bad. And although she could say that good things had come out of it, they were no thanks to her, and I was not condoning her action by receiving the gift.

Some people made helpful and encouraging comments. I had to get medically signed off, and the doctor said, "Why is it always the good ones that they do this to?" That was nice.

Somebody who had taught with me said, "If this happens to the strong ones, whatever happens to the others?" I replied, "Perhaps you can't call me a strong one anymore."

That was the end of my school career, but it wasn't the end of struggling with what forgiveness meant. The trite saying, "Forgive and forget," does not bear any resemblance to human experience because you can't forget something that has shattered your life. But I think there is something about learning how to remember. We have choices. We can keep the hurt alive by going back over it, always blaming the other person, and not seeing how the things they are coping with impinge on our life. Or we can choose not to keep the hurt alive. We are always scarred by these experiences, but it is better to have scars that still hurt than to have running sores that you have actually kept alive. It's both a gift of grace and an act of will to say, "I'm not going to let this go on poisoning my life." So I now think of the headmistress as a damaged person, but I don't think of her with bitterness.

The anger still comes up, but I recognize it for what it is. I could have turned into a very twisted, bitter person. But instead of just pushing the anger down, I repeat, "I'm not going to let this go on poisoning my life." Forgiveness is living with the very unpalatable truth that somebody you trusted is actually not worth trusting. It's being realistic about people and situations and saying, "If I choose to go on relating to you, I am choosing to relate to someone who is not trustworthy." But that doesn't mean there can't be a relationship. People sometimes try to forgive and say, "Don't worry, it doesn't matter." That's not really facing up to the fact. It's an evasion of the truth.

The other thing about forgiveness is that it's got to be received, and my ex-headmistress couldn't get anywhere near receiving it, or recognizing that I still cared about her as a person even though she had behaved despicably. It works both ways, though. Another part of forgiveness is recognizing my own need for it because I am by no means perfect in my dealings with people. The problem isn't just over there in someone else's life. What they are doing that hurts or almost destroys us is what we are all capable of doing. So we all need forgiveness. That's where the Christian view of forgiveness really bites, I think. We begin to grasp that we ourselves have been forgiven. We acknowledge and confess sin, and God's forgiveness sets us free. That's as true for ourselves as it is for the people who hurt or harm us.

I remember Eric Lomax, who worked on the Burmese railway during the Second World War and eventually was set free after having been tortured as a prisoner of war. He recognized that he had to track down his torturer. When Lomax finally met him, he saw that his torturer had also been damaged by the experience. The torturer said, "I haven't been able to get out of my mind the face of that person I tortured." He had spent his life since the war rehabilitating people who were damaged and hurt. Eric Lomax said, "I realized there came a point where the hating had to stop. This also was a human being in need of forgiveness."

Forgiveness may be a bit like conversion for some people, but for most of us it's a continual turning — such a big shift in mindset that you have to keep practising it. It's like learning deep down that you are precious to God. You have to keep on re-accepting that it's true because self-doubt keeps coming in.

People often think that forgiveness is the same as reconciliation — going on together. But the way to mend a broken limb isn't always to jam the broken bits together; it's sometimes to pull them apart and let something new grow. We can easily feel guilty because we haven't smoothed it all over and made it better, but in the real healing process, we don't return to what we were before: we move on. You never know quite what you are moving on to.

I think we have to be less intense about feeling that reconciliation means we are all going to be loving and together. Loving is often a matter of separating — recognizing the truth that there are some people it would be silly to trust because you make yourself vulnerable to being manipulated or abused all over again. If there is to be a renewed relationship, it has to be one that recognizes that you are like this and I am like that. For it to work, both people must have done a lot of reflecting and arrived at this point.

You also have to be careful not to say, "I'll bury the past," because that's no way of letting go of it. You can perhaps convince yourself for a while that you have let go, but not forever. I have been continually surprised that the old hurt is still there. Every so often something triggers it, and there it is. I think pain is a very deep well and you never really get to the bottom of it.

Forgiveness is God's gift, not something I earn by identifying sin and saying, "Sorry." I think sometimes that forgiveness comes before confession. Penitence isn't a matter of looking at myself and saying how awful I am; that just locks me into myself. Penitence is a response to the God who says, "You are precious and honoured and loved, and nothing you can do can stop me loving you." You have to respond over and over again, but each time it reaches deeper. It's really knowing, "God loves me," and learning to look for God in others that releases forgiveness in relationship. I haven't in any way earned it, but believing that I am loved has made a great difference to the way I treat myself.

If God loves me as I am, then who am I to say that I am not actually loveable? That in itself leads to joy, thanksgiving, and penitence as well.

Letting Go

Amy's Story

For me, the feeling of being forgiven is the feeling of liberation, as if a big weight has been lifted out of my chest. And although I am getting a bit old for this, I could skip or jump up and down. It's the opposite when you feel you've done something to somebody or to God: every part of you seems to drag along, the physical part, the spiritual part, and the mental part.

As the Lord's Prayer emphasizes, in order to feel truly forgiven ourselves, we must be willing to forgive. There have been times in my own life when I have withheld forgiveness or said very glibly, "Oh yes, of course I forgive you," but at the same time I know very well that a bit of me is hugging the grievance and thinking, "Aha, I've got something against you, and you still have to make it up." This causes a kind of heaviness, a general malaise that stops up the spiritual energy. In turn, it prevents me from feeling forgiven and makes me feel like a victim. Although that may give some satisfaction, it's not a healthy way to look at life.

Forgiveness is like a movement of the heart toward the other person, but in order to operate, it must be fully and openly accepted. Sometimes it's hard to accept that you're being forgiven. You feel a bit stupid and resentful that it has to be done to you. Forgiving ourselves, I think, is the hardest thing to do because whoever we are, we all get "down" periods in our lives. For me, they come when I think of things I should have done or should have done differently. These are things I regret, knowing I can never turn back the clock.

My mum died very suddenly and very unexpectedly. The last time I went to see her was a couple of days before she died. She always came out on the doorstep to wave goodbye, and feeling a bit cross and out of sorts that day, I gave her one brisk wave and shot off down the road. Ever since then I have regretted that I didn't turn and wave again.

My brother had committed suicide a few years before that. After he died, I felt very angry toward him. Now I feel ashamed of that. But at the time, what some people would call my inner child was screaming, "Thanks very much! You skipped off the scene and left me to clean up the mess." The grief came later, but the anger came first. About eighteen months before my brother died, we had a bit of a disagreement, and I find it hard to forgive myself that I didn't keep in touch more.

I would dearly love to say Sorry to these people. When these old regrets come to mind, I try to offer up a prayer for forgiveness. Sometimes I sit in church alone for an hour or more, and I find that praying helps me to move forward. When I was younger, I used to think, "How could such a nice person as me do these things?" Now I'm gradually getting more confidence to say, "Well, this is me, warts and all. I will do the best with what I have been given, because that is what I should be doing."

I want to say something about forgiveness after my husband left. We had been married for eighteen years and he suddenly went off one day to be with somebody else. I was bewildered because there hadn't been any hint of what was going to happen — or at least I hadn't noticed any. Many people suddenly appeared out of the woodwork and in the neighbourhood, who had been in the same situation. Some people, my relatives in particular, were very up in arms about the whole thing, and I suppose I felt the same way. But in a weird sort of way I felt slightly relieved because I think at rock bottom I had known something was wrong.

But I was angry. I got some old dishes, went outside, and threw them at the garage wall. That gave me a wicked feeling of satisfaction. For two or three weeks I was out every night, digging furiously in my vegetable patch. I found that very therapeutic because it used a lot of adrenaline. Even more important, I found that, when I was throwing up the earth, I was also throwing thoughts and reflections out of my head. Besides that, I had very supportive friends who helped me by listening. Some of them have a wonderful sense of humour, and whenever I felt very depressed about him leaving, I thought of them and laughed.

Later on, while I was on holiday, I sat down one day and wrote to my husband about all the good things we had had together and thanked him, saying how glad I was that we had spent those years together. After the holiday he came to see me. He thanked me for the letter and spoke about the things he had enjoyed about being with me.

Now, although neither of us used the word "forgiveness," I think there was a certain amount of forgiveness in that. It was a kind of equal forgiveness exercise that really helped both of us. Although I have seen him once or twice since, I don't feel we are any longer carrying emotional baggage because we have cleared the ground between us. It didn't involve anything like saying,

"It was my fault," or "It was your fault." It was just celebrating what we had had together and forgiving each other without actually using the word. It almost seemed to be a ceremony or ritual that we had to go through.

Reflection

Reaching Inward

When we are hurt by someone, anger is the natural response. Anger is not wrong; it is part of our God-given makeup to defend ourselves in an uncertain world. But what do we do with it?

Anger is a potent brew. For years I was afraid of my anger, assuming that expressions of anger were necessarily destructive. Therapists and others advise us to get in touch with our feelings, recognize them for what they are, and accept them. But that is not enough. Getting in touch with the energy of anger may be a healthy first step, but it does not direct the expression of that energy. We are quite capable of turning the anger on ourselves in ways that deny and destroy any sense of self-worth. We can hold onto our anger in ways that focus on destruction and end in bitterness, demanding that the world be there for our wants and needs, and nursing the anger as a way of life because the world is not organized for our benefit. Nursing anger is a way of saying, "I am in the right." It can become addictive, as the only strong feeling left to give us a sense of being ourselves.

To befriend our anger and to direct its energy into creative responses is another matter altogether. The first step is understanding that anger is there to defend our integrity. The lives of

Marian and her family, Joy, and Amy have been deeply affected by people who betrayed their trust and violated them.

Marian's rage was triggered by what happened to Lucy and to the whole family, but it also led her to recognize her own capacities for destructive behaviour, and that led her into a deeper understanding of the darkness that had assaulted them all.

Joy felt dismantled, betrayed, publicly humiliated. Her anger appeared naturally and strongly, and it saved her from crumbling under the experience. It defended her self-respect. She then had to struggle over a long period of time, daily refusing to let it poison her life, refusing to take on the role of a victim, using the anger to focus on the truth of what had happened without condoning it. Continually surprised by the strong feelings of hurt and rage triggered by the memories, she had to recognize repeatedly that to succumb to the temptation to seek revenge would entrench the rage, collude with the pattern of inflicting hurt where hurt had been received, and so make it far more difficult ever to grow through the experience herself.

The temptation to nurse anger bitterly can be very strong, but it is a trap. Instead Joy used the energy of the anger to strengthen her courage to face the hurt and deal with it creatively. There was no pretending that everything was all right, that "things worked out for the best." When hurt runs deep, to "forgive and forget" is a denial of the reality. Things have changed, and relationships can never go back to being what they were before.

The second step is to attempt to listen to the inner person whom the anger is defending. Anger is a defence when we are deeply wounded. The noise of anger is so loud, energetic, and exhausting that it is hard to hear the hurt person inside ourselves who is vulnerable, fearful, asking whether it is possible to trust anyone. Although the hurting self wants to be heard and respected, it takes courage to admit to the hurt, and we usually need people who we can trust, who can hold us when we are permitting the hurt to be expressed.

Alongside the pain, there is often a sense of shame. To whom can I admit that my life has been violated? And then, when the rage inside shows us our own capacity for destruction, we may feel ashamed and afraid of its power. Many perpetrators of abuse also carry a sense of shame at what they have done. Living with the fact can drive them to despair. Doris Klein comments,

> So often, we fear being seen in our truth and desperately try to hide what we perceive as inadequacy. We cloak ourselves with efforts to please, produce, and perform, hoping our efforts will be enough. We cling to the covers of power or proficiency as we attempt to avoid being seen in our vulnerability.... We work hard at earning love, grasping for what we fear we don't deserve, ashamed of who we are because we have, for so long, believed that we don't measure up.
>
> Shame escalates in the dark. As we hold it within and fail to give it a voice, it grows, sapping our energy and power. Shame, however, cannot survive in the light because truth melts the lies that sustain it. To release our shame, we must name it; we must peel back the layers and masks behind which we have hidden for so long. We simply ask for the grace to stand in the Presence of Unbounded Love, who peels away these old and sticky patterns.
>
> Naming and letting go of these layers can be painstakingly slow, demanding a discipline of honesty, courage, and

patience to be faithful. This is not a place to rush but a process of walking step by step, not missing a beat, honouring the learning as each layer falls away. We often seek soul-companions along this walk, those who can stand with us, gently encouraging us and witnessing with compassion as we remove the masks. In that safe space we can assume a position of honesty, allowing ourselves to see the truth. In this process we are continually invited to come home to ourselves. As we become more attentive to the voice of our heart, the long-held lies fall aside, and we are able to stand in the truth and beauty of who we are.[1]

Klein has described much of the process of forgiving ourselves both for being violated and for being who we are. But how do we forgive another person who neither seeks nor desires it?

For Joy, forgiveness began with recognizing the truth that someone she had trusted could not be trusted, and that trust might not be restored. Then she had to let go of the rage that would destroy, and by letting go (which may require doing so many times) she found she could be freed from bondage to the wound. That is not easy, and Joy drew strength from her mature Christian faith. It led her to a deeper appreciation of the fact that God loves us first, and nothing we do can stop that. We cannot earn God's love, and we do not have to, but many of us take a surprisingly long time to realize this. Responding to

---

1   Doris Klein, CSA, *Journey of the Soul* (Franklin, Wisconsin: Sheed and Ward, 2000), pp. 95ff.

that love, realizing that we need it, can release compassion for one who has hurt us. Gradually the letting go takes place and we are healed, whether or not the other has said Sorry at all.

As Joy said to me in another context, "Forgiveness isn't about being let off, it's about being set free. Jesus didn't let people off; he offered forgiveness. But there was a cost — the cost of changing."

Personal Forgiveness

Early Wounds

Beginnings

My earliest memories of childhood are a jumble, like snapshots without labels or dates. At home, near Toronto. Learning to tie my shoelaces. The sun coming through the window onto the kitchen table at breakfast. Tonsils out on the kitchen table at the age of four (I think it was during the Second World War).

What I cannot remember is my birth, and in spite of all the marvellous images we are now given of conception and the development of a child in the womb, I cannot really think of my beginning. I am in the middle of my life, not knowing its beginning or end. I may not be here tomorrow; life is uncertain and transient. The awareness of transience can make us conscious of each day as provisional — a gift of possibilities in a world that is precious and fragile. It can also create deep anxiety.

Scientists are now trying to establish mathematical models of the universe, describing its basic dynamics right back to the first three seconds or so of its existence. We can ask, What was there at the beginning, before the big bang? But the question has no meaning. Einstein has taught us that space and time are interlocked, that one does not exist without the other. Both are part of the process of creation.

In fact, St. Augustine realized this sixteen hundred years ago when writing a meditation on time in his book, *Confessions*. The opening words of the Bible, "In the beginning God created …," describe the profound truth that space, time, force, matter, life, relationship, and all the rest emerge in the act of creation. We can ask where it all happened, but this question too has no meaning. There was no "where" until creation occurred. Even the words I am using now take their meaning from within the created order and have no meaning outside it. We cannot imagine the beginning of creation without putting it in the middle of a space-time framework that only exists at the "time" of the big bang.

The Bible's first sentence tells of God acting in freedom to bring the universe into existence. The Bible's story of creation is not a scientific description, but an unfolding of our place in creation. We emerge from God's act of freedom with a capacity to respond to our creator. A free act that confers freedom also calls for trust. As we discover how fragile we are, how dependent we are on this world and our relations with others, we recognize that living calls for trust. Can we trust God, who is within but beyond creation and beyond our understanding?

I cannot imagine my own birth, even after watching the birth of my children. Memory cannot penetrate that far. I was conceived through the free act of my parents. I was born totally dependent on people I did not know. Could I trust them? From conception onwards I was emerging from non-being into being a person. At birth I became a separate human being with a unique identity more potential than actual, essentially alone and totally vulnerable, dependent upon others for survival and nurture. Slowly I emerged as a person through the relationships of family, friends, and community in God's world.

Alongside the practical needs for food, housing, warmth, and protection, what I needed as a child was the empathetic understanding of others so that I might come to see, understand, and respect the fragments that were slowly being formed into my personhood. Through these needs being met, I came to understand what being loved is about.

But the care that a young child receives is given by people who are imperfectly formed themselves, who carry wounds within their own histories. We pass on imperfections whether we want to or not, because none of us, individually or together, is capable of meeting the full needs of a child. I remember growing up as an anxious child, and I did not want to pass on to my children the wound of deep anxiety. Of course, I failed. I may have been a "good enough" parent, as were my own parents. But the early wounds we carry, even though we may be unaware of them, affect the formation of our characters and our behaviour. Children absorb them early. I remember overhearing our young children scolding their dolls in precisely the same words and tones that we used with them.

What then happens when children suffer wounding from people they are asked to trust? There are the obvious assaults such as sexual abuse, overt violence, physical or emotional abandonment by one or both parents. There are the less obvious assaults such as the needs of the caregivers dominating everything — needs like addictions, emotional demands, or constant unresolved conflicts. A child finds such traumas difficult indeed to handle, let alone forgive. Here are some stories of the struggle to cope with such early experiences.

Paralysis

Bruce's Story

M y mother was a powerful person, centred round herself. Her attitude to my sister and me depended considerably on whether we were a credit to her or not. She wanted to enjoy life as much as possible, and while expecting us to be obedient and clever, she wanted us to avoid making any demands on her, financial or emotional. Displays of affection were not encouraged in our family.

My sister was made to leave school at sixteen, and since the Second World War was in progress, she was evacuated almost at once because of her job in the Civil Service. She never returned home. She died of cancer at the age of fifty-five, and in her last weeks we talked quite a lot about our childhood and our mother. She felt there had been totally unreachable expectations all the time and that, no matter what she did, Mother always expected something better. She was sure that Mother never knew she was sometimes being cruel, but I believe Mother could be deliberately cruel. My sister had avoided contact with Mother after her marriage; in fact, at one point her husband refused to let her see her Mother because she was so upset by her. Mother came to see my sister once as she was dying and brought her some flowers, and afterwards dissolved into tears that she soon suppressed. My sister died saying, "It isn't fair."

There was no recognition of a need for forgiveness on either side. Mother's power paralysed my sister. If a deliberate attempt at rapprochement isn't made at some point during life, there's too much to do when you are at death's door! I am sure bitterness, distress, and disappointment can make you ill and maybe even give you cancer. If you never come to terms with everything inside yourself — that is, if you never forgive in your imagination — then you can't do it in fact or face to face. The wrong will wrap round and round you like the web a spider spins to wrap up a fly, so that progress becomes impossible and the sense of grievance hinders all aspects of life. It becomes obsessional and very sad.

It seems to me that in families there has to be a continuing sense of forgiving, and also of being forgiven for all our shortcomings. If this doesn't happen, a situation builds to almost impossible proportions without being recognized, as with my sister. It's not easy to change behaviour inside a family and to reconcile very different personalities. But accepting differences is a way to start.

A Glass Wall

Amanda's Story

My brother is nearly three years older than I am. My earliest memories of him, when I was around two, are of his becoming uncontrollably violent to me and also to my parents. They couldn't seem to control him. Even at that age he had a lot of power over me, so it was difficult to refuse to do anything he wanted. For example, he and his friend would tie me up in my doll's carriage and drag me all round the local recreation ground and over the railway lines and down by the river. I never knew whether they were going to put me over the waterfall. He could reduce me to screams of terror just by taking off his glasses and staring at me.

From about the time when I was five or six, it seemed to me that, whenever my brother did anything right, he got praise and he grew to expect this. Whenever I did anything right — passed an exam or anything — I was told it was expected of me. It seemed he was a lot more important than I was.

His violence toward me got worse, and it started to become sexual. Looking back now, I feel certain that he himself must have been abused at that age, probably by my father who, I think, was by inclination homosexual. My father had married probably because it was what one did to cover up an alternative sexuality. My brother at the age of eight or nine suddenly started forcing oral sex on me and threatened me if I told anybody.

My mother died when I was nine, but she had never been able to protect me from the violence. My brother was very clever with electronics. I remember that once he put ring-style electrodes onto my fingers when my mother was present, and even when he closed the circuit and I got a terrible shock, she did nothing about it.

By the time I was about eleven or twelve, my brother brought in friends who also used me as a sex object. I could see no way out of it. I worried about whether I was going to become pregnant, but I just couldn't tell anybody. At this stage I would run away frequently to my aunt and uncle's just to get away from the situation. One New Year's Eve, when things had got particularly bad, I walked the twelve miles in deep snow to get there. I never told them why, and they never asked. They always took me in without asking any questions or showing any surprise. At first they used to phone my father every time and tell him where I was, and he would come immediately and take me back. Later they just let me stay. Once my aunt refused to let my uncle phone my father, saying, "We'll wait to see how long it takes him to ring us this time." After a couple of weeks they gave up and let him know. His response was, "I thought she'd be there." He hadn't even checked that I was still attending school, which I was. I could have been anywhere.

One day I walked in and found my father with another man. He tried to force me to swear on Bibles that I had never seen anything. My brother moved out before he was seventeen. After he left, he wrote very infrequently and came home less frequently, but one year in February he suddenly arrived. By this time I was at college, and my uncle turned up there to collect me; this had never happened before. On the way home he told me that my father had been arrested. Later that day he was brought home, having been prescribed tranquillizers. I was the one who had to dish them out. My brother stayed the weekend, but he left the next week, and that was the last time I saw him. There I was as a teenager, trying to handle all this without being able to share it with anyone. I found that, whenever I started to trust someone and tell them a bit about my family background, they disappeared. So I rapidly came to the conclusion that you just don't let anybody know.

I'm angry — with my brother definitely — and with my parents for not protecting me. They should have been able to protect a small child at least, even if they couldn't do it when I was older. I'm also angry at the consequences — the continuing lack of trust I have in other people. Since then I have been able to tell a few people the story, but I have never let them get close to me. It's like living inside a glass wall. I still can't reach through. It's too frightening to the real me who is inside the wall. I am in touch with the real me, and it is very difficult. There are lots of times when I can feel almost like a caged animal backing into the cage, away from someone.

What would I do if I met my brother again? I don't know. He's the one I can't forgive. He's the one I felt as a child that I ought to be able to trust more than anybody else. But I couldn't.

I have been able to forgive other people. It took me a long time, but when my father died, I could forgive him for the way he had abused me. I don't think he ever realized that I held him guilty of anything. I saw him more as a sad, confused man who was trapped into a way of life that wasn't natural for him. When

I was sixteen and still at home, he came home drunk one night and raped me. I looked very much like my mother, and he even called me by my mother's name the whole time. I made sure it never happened again. I don't even know whether he knew he did it. I never dared bring the subject up. He would probably have totally denied it the way he totally denied his homosexuality. When he died, it was a feeling of relief for me and for him that finally the whole of his troubled life was over.

I think I've forgiven most of this — the neglect, the lack of understanding. They weren't wilful on his part, whereas what I received from my brother was always calculated, wilful malice, designed to bring out terror. It's not pleasant as a child to have somebody hold you down and pour caustic soda over your hands and arms, and then have to find some reason to explain the burns away because you can't tell what actually happened. There was a collusion of silence. There is still a deep terror inside that prevents me from forgiving my brother. I am paralysed by it. I wish I could let it go.

Released

Jane's Story

I suppose the biggest mistake I have made was to leave a marriage to which I thought I was committed. For years I refused to forgive myself, until gradually it dawned on me that the lack of self-forgiveness was preventing a new life from taking root. Then I became able to look at the marriage and subsequent divorce in a different way. Being able to reflect on what went wrong and who was responsible for what, gave me the strength to acknowledge the mistakes, the lack of love, and the pain of it all. That made new beginnings possible.

It has not been easy to forgive myself, but with age has come a little wisdom. Accepting that I am never going to get life one hundred per cent right no matter how hard I try, is a step toward forgiving myself. For many years it mattered that people could accept me, even when they knew I had left a husband and children. Eventually I met and married my present husband, and he has been wonderfully loving and supportive. Thanks to him and to other caring people, I have been forced to look at myself again. Constant prayer and reflection have given me the courage to reach out.

Others have forgiven me much earlier than I have forgiven myself. I am so self-critical. The criticism from my childhood has had a deep impact on how I perceive myself. Forgiving myself has meant trying to let go of the drive for approval and perfection, and letting go of trying to make people accept me or forgive me. Forgiving myself is a part of accepting myself as I am, of seeing myself as God's work of art.

An experience of being forgiven came from my son before he went to Bangladesh for a year. He gave me a letter just before he left. He had written about how, since he was about twelve, he had watched me and had begun to understand how much I had given up in order to survive and love him after the separation from his father. He said that, when he had become old enough to understand, he knew there was no point in blaming either me or his father, but that something deeper had caused the divorce. He knew that he was very deeply loved, and somehow he knew that he had not been rejected. Because the letter was given with such love, and because for all his youth he had seen right into the heart of me, I was able to accept it and cherish it.

I think this was the real beginning of the process of forgiving my father. Until very recently I was certain that I would never be able to forgive him for his irresponsibility and violence during my childhood and adolescence. His regular physical attacks on my mother, and the constant verbal belittling of her and all of us children, left a hard core of pain and anger within me. To release them from my heart would seem like a betrayal of the hurt. I understand intellectually the reasons for his behaviour, and for years I prayed, thought, raged, and wept, convincing myself that I had forgiven him. However, in my heart I knew this was not so, because the draining of energy was still so apparent when I heard his voice or was in his presence, and I felt that only his death would give me freedom.

As the years went by, the anger became diluted but the pain increased. I knew that by not forgiving him I was continuing to punish myself — my whole life was polluted. It felt like carrying a stone inside, a huge paralysis. Yet the experience of loving and being loved has given me the courage to carry on trying. Even when my father refused contact with me, I kept the contact alive. This is where the Spirit was able to really work within me. Recently when my father sent me flowers for my birthday, I felt he was reaching out to me. Then one morning he telephoned and talked about dying and about his grandchildren, but without making any demands. I decided that I would go to see him. It was a momentous time for both of us, and he hugged me longer than he ever had before. As I left, he took my face between his hands and stared at me. The stone inside dissolved.

The long, long struggle has led me to a deeper understanding of him, myself, and forgiveness. I saw in him the terrified little boy who had learned that the only way to survive was to fight. On an intellectual level I had always known this about him, but that morning I saw the reality of the child. Now it feels that the poison has drained away from my life. I have told him calmly my feelings about our life as a family. And I have told him that I love him. Forgiving him released love and compassion — that came as a revelation.

Reflection

Healing Early Wounds

When a child is born, the new parents have to learn what bringing up a child requires. Since no parents get it entirely right, all children receive wounds to their emerging personalities. Many children cope very well; some do not. But all absorb the attitudes and expectations of their parents (and of the wider community) long before they realize it.

When parents' expectations reflect their own needs rather than the child's possibilities, the child may be afflicted with guilt at being unable to meet the expectations. This guilt may persist into adulthood. Like Bruce's sister, we can die trying to live out — or rebel against — parental expectations. We need the love of others to help detach ourselves from unreal expectations. Such detaching can feel like learning to forgive ourselves for being who we are and not who others would like us to be. Is forgiveness the right word? Certainly we need to learn how to take on responsibility for our own decisions and behaviour. But as we grow, the question "Who am I?" faces us all. How de we come accept ourselves as unique and God-gifted persons? It may mean shedding those unreal expectations that we didn't know we were carrying. Almost certainly it includes shedding any false self-images that we have constructed to cope with the world, and allowing a more true self to emerge. It may include coming to terms with parts of our character and life-history that are deeply painful. Such growth usually takes a long time, and it can feel like purgation. Ann and Barry Ulanov comment:

There occurs that first stripping away of the false, of mere appearance, of cover-ups and counterfeit poses which seal us off from our true selves and from God. Whatever hounds us that we despise, or fear, or despair over, will turn up in these moments for prayerful consideration with God. Here we are scoured, stripped bare of the myriad deceits, large and small, that infiltrate our being. Painfully, our values, even our best — our esteem of justice, love, health, peace for ourselves and our world — are often exposed as values held with such possessive force that they have built a wall in us against the force of God's will.

Purgation really surprises us. It turns things around in both psyche and soul. It is not just castigation. And it may be more difficult to take than any mere chastening, for it requires accepting ourselves and sometimes accepting that what superficially looks like a fault or limitation, even a sin, may turn out to be a major part of our identity, even an opening through which God reaches right into us. There, in our own special way, no matter how lowly, we can become part of the sodden earth in which Christ appears. Thus a deep wound to the formation of an ego, that centre of personal identity, that might leave us forever fragile, anxious, boarded up against others, may instead become the aperture, the very point of sure accessibility through which

God touches the soul and moves it to give all its needs and hopes into God's care.[1]

Many people with terribly painful early wounds have no conscious memory of what happened. The memory is blocked deep inside, while the pain remains, affecting behaviour and attitudes in ways that are not easy to understand. Recovering such memories, though costly and difficult, is the key to freeing oneself from their grip.

Amanda, the victim of prolonged abuse, feels like a frightened, hurting child behind a glass wall. Neither her father nor her brother has admitted responsibility, while other close people seem helpless before the collusion of silence. Understanding her father has eased the anger against him somewhat, but the glass wall remains in place. It helps her to cope with a world she cannot trust by preventing people from getting close to her. It also helps to shut her off from the trauma of terror, assault, abuse, and rape, the degradation of personhood. But she is trapped behind the wall by the fear of entering the pain of those wounds once again. She has learned to trust a few people, but there are no fast releases here, and forgiving the perpetrators may or may not happen in this life.

But what about those who are responsible for giving abuse? Here is the story of someone I shall call Peter.

---

1 Ann and Barry Ulanov, "Prayer and Personality: Prayer as Primary Speech," in Cheslyn Jones, Geoffrey Wainwright, Edward Yarnold, S.J., eds., *The Study of Spirituality* (New York: Oxford University Press, 1986), p. 28ff.

Restoration?

Peter's Story

S ome years ago I was looking after some children. I was very
friendly with them, and I got a bit carried away and played
some rather rude games with them. This carried on for quite
some time, and they obviously told their mum. I had a visit
from the police. They arrested me and bailed me, but I went
through loads and loads of court cases. My barrister said that I
wouldn't get a heavy sentence because the offence wasn't serious
enough; there was nothing physical with these children. But I
did. In the Crown Court they sentenced me to a custodial sentence of nine months. It was an absolute nightmare, but
obviously I had to be punished for what I had done.

In prison I got very depressed, wanting to take my own life.
I made numerous attempts, which I'm not proud of now. So I
was put into the hospital for my own safety. I landed in a strip
cell for people who try to cause self-harm. There's nothing in
there, and you can't do harm to yourself — bang your head on
the wall or whatever. My idea was just to get back out again. In
the end they transferred me over to another ward, and I met a
lot of people in there who had done things three times worse
than I had.

When I was in the ward, I started to go to the chapel just to
get out of my cell. In the end, chapel seemed something I could

get on with. I let my mum visit me in the prison and told her that I was thinking of becoming a Christian. My mum's not a believer, and she just shut it off. But I kept going, getting more into it. I got on well with the prison chaplain. And I found people I could talk to. I even made friends in spite of what they were in for. You have to make friends; otherwise you don't get on. It's a very nasty place.

When I came out, I went back to where I used to live, but a neighbour made my life a misery. So I loaded up the car and went to my mum's temporarily. Then I moved here — the first time, into temporary housing. I started coming to church and got to know quite a few people. I managed to tell a few people about my background. Then the council found me a permanent flat elsewhere. I got on quite well there until somebody found out about my background, and they turned against me and made my life miserable. Sometimes I still made attempts on my life. I loaded up the car again, kept the place going just to store big stuff, and went back to my mum's and waited for some time. Then when I came back here again, it really made me quite happy.

I used to drive over to a judo club in the town where the family lives where I got into trouble. The kids saw my car and threw bricks at every single window. It really upset me because the only hobby I've got is my car. I used to see a friend at judo, but somebody told him about my background, and he said he didn't want to know me anymore, and he wanted me away from the place because he had children himself.

I have settled here, and many people are friendly. But just recently a guy shouted out obscenities to me near where I live, and I really felt depressed. I feel that I should be able to get on with my life now, not be always persecuted after all this time. I ended up calling the doctor, telling him how I felt. He came and gave me some sleeping tablets. At the moment I often go over to my mum's during the day because, as soon as I step out the door of my place, people's eyes are looking, and I am just waiting for someone to shout something out. Many people here have forgiven me, but there are still a lot of people who haven't. I expected this for a year or two after I came out, but not after that. I regret terribly what I did, but I can't turn back the clock. I know in my own heart that God has forgiven me, but the people who aren't willing to forgive are making my life very tough.

People say you have to forgive yourself. I find it's one of the real hardest things to do. How can you forgive yourself when you've hurt children? In time, maybe. It helps when I know that other people forgive me. But that's a very slow process. Obviously I have to trust somebody quite a lot before I can tell them, and yes, I've told quite a lot of people here, and that's probably a mistake. The priest has been good. He tells me off when I try any of my lies. I do a lot at the church, and I also help in a seniors' day-centre. When I was first asked about helping, I was unsure because of my background, but then I looked at it and said, "Hey, it's not children; it's adults I'd be dealing with," and if I can help these people, then I will.

Many people have been very supportive, but there are still a few who shout obscenities, and I don't mind telling you, it's terrifying, because I don't want to get pressured again. I want my life to go on, looking at the bright side of things. I haven't tried taking my own life for quite some time. As I say, I've never been proud of doing that. But I can feel the release from God. It's a great comfort to know that and to believe it.

Reflection

Community Responses

The attitudes of communities and society matter more than we like to admit. Of course, every community needs boundaries in order to maintain a sense of identity. But are they boundaries of fear or inclusion?

When a person convicted of child abuse is released from prison, often there is an outcry from the neighbourhood where he is known to have settled. I have no doubt about the right to express moral anger when it is truly felt. When you, or someone in your family or local community, has been violated in some way, anger is a natural response, and moral anger at a particular evil can be very healthy. Indeed, when a society gets so used to theft or mugging or murder that it shrugs its shoulders with indifference, that society is clearly in a bad way.

Legal punishment can be a social expression of moral anger against a convicted person. But prison can also be a place where rehabilitation of the prisoner might begin. Having done his term, will communities accept him back? Is he going to be allowed to re-enter society, and if so, how? If not, what is to happen? Can we allow communities to give their own sentence of life imprisonment?

When Peter came out of prison, he discovered that the family of the victims continued to be very angry with him over the abuse of their children. The sense of invasion, violation, and betrayal remained strong. They had to struggle to absorb the energy of their anger and direct it creatively; otherwise they were in danger of being trapped in the anger, which would then become unhealthy for them. They were not yet ready to forgive Peter, nor did Peter ask it of them. Forgiveness requires truth, and it is not clear whether Peter has truly recognized and acknowledged what he has done. He knows he has done something that others understand to be wrong, and he wants to turn away from it. But without an accepting community around him to keep him on the straight and narrow, his good intentions may not be enough to prevent a relapse.

The reaction of many, when they find out about his past, is an angry revulsion that can take the form of verbal abuse or even physical threats. These people have not suffered personally from his actions and do not know the details, but they express a social anger of rejection. This response may be natural, especially among those responsible for children themselves, but it is very easy to form prejudicial attitudes in the heart that prevent us from seeing the offender as a human being. The temptation then is to enjoy rejecting another, whether it be for their colour, beliefs, gender, or for their offence. The prejudice protects us against facing the possibility that we too, being human, are capable of behaving in the same way as the person we are rejecting.

Social anger also comes from fear. We live in a society with a strong emphasis on the isolated individual and nuclear family. As every parent bringing up children knows, we cannot be sure what values we share with others, and whether the values we pass on to our children will find support in the wider society. The society will be weakened if there is a lack of commonly held values. In such circumstances, when a community is faced with an outsider whom it feels unable to trust, we may be caught up in a fearful response of anger, and even violence.

Peter found acceptance from his mother, who stuck by him and took him in from time to time when he had no other place to go. The chaplaincy in prison introduced him to a God who, in the person of Christ, could see him truly as he was and, by loving him in his weakness and sinfulness, could open him up to the possibility of change. For Peter, recognizing that God forgave him did not mean pretending that his offences were not so bad after all. It meant facing, without being rejected, the reality of what he had done. Getting to this point was a slow process, because often one can face only a little reality at a time. The seed of possibility was planted in prison, and the seed was nurtured effectively when Peter discovered a church community that had a strong sense of its own identity, faith, and purpose.

The church and its leadership could receive Peter without fear and with a perceptive understanding of the boundaries he needed. Peter was honest enough with the leadership for them to be honest with him about the need to protect the children, without rejecting him. Even more important, he discovered ways of contributing creatively to the church community while recognizing the need never to be alone with children. The church worked out its own expression of forgiveness without maintaining a naive trust that demanded more than Peter could give. The church was sufficiently secure in its own cohesion and identity to enfold Peter gently and truthfully, and so gave expression to God's forgiveness. The wider, more disparate community could not always do this, and so has made it far more difficult for Peter to forgive himself.

The very act that damages another also damages ourselves, fractures our integrity, and makes us morally blind. Coming to appreciate that we are forgiven, and that we can forgive ourselves, is a slow, cyclical process. By cyclical, I mean that receiving some love and acceptance helps us to grow in inner strength, so that we can face more of the truth of what we have done or failed to do. We see more, grow a little more in integrity, take on more of the truth and more responsibility for our actions, and realize our need for a deeper forgiveness. If this cycle of growth takes place within a stable, accepting community, then the growth has the quality of hope. But if there is no such community, coming to a deeper realization of our offence can easily lead to despair. Peter attempted suicide many times, especially when he had to face the truth in the context of rejection and isolation.

Moral anger has its place, in both individuals and society. But we are all fragile creatures who find it easier to use such anger destructively and fearfully rather than creatively. Used thus, social anger ceases to be moral, seeking someone to blame when things go wrong. "Lock them up and throw away the key," we think. Thus the prison population grows, fear and anger remain, and nothing is healed. It seems to be true that some people convicted of child abuse, for their own protection as well as ours, need to be confined for a long time. However, this is not true for many of those so convicted.

What about Peter? Does he need to be confined for a long time? Probably not, though a fearful community would say he should be. His story showed me society's destructive capacity, but it also showed the importance of Christian communities being places where forgiveness is experienced among people more ready to enfold a sinner gently, with clear eyes on both the truth of the situation and the creative possibilities. I believe we all need to be seen as having the potential to change.

Can Peter grow sufficiently to receive and trust loving acceptance, and for how long and how deeply? For him to believe and accept forgiveness, and so eventually forgive himself, will be a lengthy process. He heard the church community saying to him, "Come in and rest a while," but other people were still shouting hate at him. It is not clear whether the steady voices of acceptance will prevail when the harsh voices are so easily amplified.

Community Forgiveness

Conflict in Northern Ireland

Conflict in Northern Ireland

I n Northern Ireland I lived for a while on a "peace line" between two hostile rcommunities. My stay in Belfast led me
to appreciate the way people there quietly live lives from which
understanding and respect can grow. Struggling through times
of suffering in their families and communities as creatively as
possible, they try to break down the barriers of fear and stereotypes. Their struggle is not just against personal attitudes, but
also against communal attitudes of "them" and "us" that per-
vade Northern Ireland.

I was told that in Northern Ireland two questions are suffi-
cient to "place" a person: "What is your name? Where did you
go to school?" Although mixed schools are developing now
(driven by the wish of parents), most schools are denomina-
tionally based, and many families still encourage their children
to go to the school of their denomination. The Roman Catholic and the Protestant communities are similar in many respects,
yet the similarity seems to lead them to emphasize their differences even more vehemently. Alan Falconer reflects that history
holds each community captive.

Among the Protestant communities there is a "siege men-
tality." Protestants tend to remember those occasions in their

history when they had been under siege from Roman Catholic forces. Thus the [Protestant] history lessons emphasize 1641 when the Catholic Earls rose against the Protestants to try to reclaim the land given to the incomers [i.e., Protestant settlers imported by the English].

Even more notable was the siege of Derry in 1690 (still commemorated annually by the Apprentice Boys Parade), when the exiled Roman Catholic King James II tried to regain his throne in England by invading Ireland and losing to the new king, the Protestant William of Orange. Correspondingly,

> there exists a "coercion mentality" among Roman Catholics — a sense of being colonized and of having freedom limited by another community. Within this coercion mentality is a memory that independence and freedom have had to be sought through force of arms.... The cohesiveness and sense of direction of the community is nourished by its memories.... The identity of each community [has] been shaped by the actions, attitudes and declarations of other communities. Both siege and coercion mentalities are reactions to the actions of others. The definition of each has been crafted over and against "the other."[1]

The past is always present. The two communities share one long history, but by defining themselves over against each other, they demonize the other, see the other only in stereotypes, and blame

---

1 Alan D. Falconer and Joseph Liechty, eds., *Reconciling Memories* (Dublin: Columba Press, 1998), p.11ff.

the other for everything that is wrong. Violence is always on the agenda. Communities that define themselves by their own history tend to write that history in ways that reinforce their own sense of identity, attitudes, and values. Any other version of history is rejected as biased.

The legacy of history in Northern Ireland, where the common inheritance of Christian faith is greater than the differences that divide Protestant and Roman Catholic interpretations of it, has interlocked religious differences with political differences and differences of social class. The Protestant community, with its long history of support from Great Britain, calls itself "Loyalist" or "Unionist"— a reference to its determination to ensure that Northern Ireland remains part of the United Kingdom so that they may continue to receive protection from Britain. In the Roman Catholic community, the many who would prefer union with the Republic of Ireland are called Republicans.

Both Protestants and Roman Catholics are aware that Protestants have long held certain social and economic advantages. Both sides have raised their own unofficial armies — the paramilitaries, "paras" for short. On the Catholic side, the Irish Republican Army was an old organization, but it developed a new arm, the Provisional IRA, and it relied on the Sinn Fein to represent it politically. On the Protestant side there were paramilitary groups such as the Ulster Defence Army, the UDA.

Michael Ignatieff, in his book *The Warrior's Honour*, asks why communities that share so much in common turn on each other with the fiercest hostility. He notes that "the story of Cain seems to say, at its simplest, that there are no wars more savage than civil wars, no hatreds more intractable than those between closest kin."[2] He turns to the insights of Sigmund Freud, who wrote in 1917 that "it is precisely the minor differences in people who are otherwise alike that form the basis of feelings of strangeness and hostility between them."[3]

When minor differences are used as expressions of power and status by one group over another, these differences can become major. "The less substantial the differences between two groups, the more they both struggle to portray those differences as absolute. Moreover, the aggression that is required to hold a group together is not only directed outward at another group, but is directed inward at eliminating the differences that distinguish individual from group."[4] When a group so encloses itself in a circle of self-righteousness that its members cannot listen, cannot hear, cannot learn from anybody outside themselves, then listening to strangers is deemed worthless. Indeed, members of the "other" community are not really human at all. Intolerance becomes dominant.

Much of the good being done to bridge the gulf between the two communities in Northern Ireland never makes news. I came back from Belfast more encouraged than when I arrived, because of the wonderful people I had met who were working at the community level, struggling courageously and at great cost to themselves over many years against tribal definitions of people. Here are some of their stories.

---

2   Michael Ignatieff, *The Warrior's Honour: Ethnic War and the Modern Consciousness* (London: Chatto & Windus, 1998), p. 48.
3   *The Warrior's Honour*, p. 48.
4   *The Warrior's Honour*, p. 51

Journey Toward Understanding

Sam Burch's Story

I am a Methodist minister, retired now, but in 1970 I came to the Shankill Road, which is a Loyalist area here in Belfast. There was a lot of rioting, and people were being burned out of houses. A gang was operating at the top of the road. There didn't seem to be anything much that Christian groups and congregations were able to do about this situation. I had had contact previously with Catholic people through clergy fraternals and things like that, and I did not want to lose those links.

I was searching for a contact when I was approached by a Presbyterian minister saying there was a conference of Catholics in Larne. Would I gather a few people from my church? He would gather a few from his, because these Roman Catholics wanted to have some Protestant contact. We had a wonderful time sharing stories and Bible insights at that conference, and this led to a little prayer group that continued to meet through all the Troubles. There were only about five of us to start with, but it soon outgrew the Catholic sisters' house where we had been meeting, and we came then to the local Clonard Monastery just off the Falls Road. About twenty-five to thirty of us were meeting once a week there for prayer.

When the hunger strikes came in the early eighties, it was a tense, difficult time in Belfast and particularly here. People were dying week after week, and there were demonstrations and black flags and coffins being carried in the streets. We were on the verge of civil war, and field stations were set up ready to help the injured. This called us to a deeper intensity of prayer in our little group, and out of that came the idea to form a community of reconciliation and peace here in West Belfast. We managed it through the good offices of a retired Conservative MP called Sir Cyril Black, a Baptist. His Trust purchased two houses for us on the Springfield Road, which is a kind of peace line between the Falls Catholic Republican area and the Shankill Loyalist Protestant area. Four members of the group, all women, moved in to form the beginning of the Cornerstone Community.

That was in December 1982. We have been here ever since: praying, laughing, drinking cups of tea, doing ridiculous things like holding demonstrations in the middle of the street, and trying to call the two communities to begin to listen to each other. We especially want the churches to explore their faith journeys together and play a more active part in this process of reconciliation.

In the early days, through the seventies and early eighties, the churches seemed impotent because we had allowed ourselves to become trapped in the political situation, being virtually tribal churches with tribal chaplains. We were therefore unable to be the bridge of understanding and reconciliation that I am sure Jesus would call us to be.

I formed a relationship with a Catholic priest from the monastery here, Fr. Gerry Reynolds, and he and I started to visit victims of the Troubles. We went to some forty homes in this immediate neighbourhood where people had been murdered. Sometimes policemen or paramilitary people had been shot dead in their homes, and we would visit the families. It seemed to be a more healing presence when the pair of us went together, a Catholic priest and a Protestant minister. We would usually pray in the homes of the people for healing and for a way out of the dilemma. We never blamed anybody except history for falling into this tribal pattern in which each group was terrified of the other.

I remember going into one home, and the lad was lying in the coffin. The mother, a kindly motherly soul, said she had been in the house when the gunmen came to get her son. "I pleaded with them on my knees to shoot me rather than my son, but they wouldn't." Things like that were absolutely gut-wrenching, and to be able to share in prayer with the people who were suffering and tell them we would remember them in the Cornerstone Community prayers was always helpful.

There were programs of bringing children together, young people together, women's groups together, communities together. One couldn't say it has been successful because the numbers have been so small in those groups, yet it's like the grain of a mustard seed in the gospel. We are still present here between the Falls and the Shankill, and people have gotten to know that Catholics and Protestants are working together here — priests, sisters, ministers, ministers' wives, ordinary lay people from the streets. This in itself is a kind of parable or symbol or icon for the communities to look to.

I've been here now for thirty years on and off. Surviving in a place like this isn't easy. In my own church the Cornerstone Community created energy for me and was the fallback whenever the going got hard. There was always somebody's shoulder to weep on, and also somebody to show you that maybe it wasn't as bad as you thought it was, and that there was hope and light at the end of the tunnel. And the group at Clonard, with wonderful people of great faith and vision and hope and courage, has carried us through the bad times and lifted us up again whenever we got down.

Forgiving is very, very difficult. I remember the very first house that we visited where there had been murder. The son had been shot dead in the street outside, and after our sharing time, the father of the lad said to me, "I feel so angry. If I could just get my hands round their necks, it would give me the greatest delight to squeeze the life out of them, whoever did this to my son." That's the reality. How do you talk to somebody like that about forgiveness? So we didn't. We talked about God's mercy and help to get over these traumas. We've been back in touch with that family a number of times, and I think a certain amount of healing has taken place, but I don't believe that that man could forgive. The rage is still there.

Sometimes it becomes more bitter. Another woman said, "I look out my window on a Saturday night, and I see the couples all gathering to go down to the club for a drink, and I have no partner because they murdered him." Others seem to get an amazing miraculous grace to almost immediately forgive the people who did it. I don't know how they do it. I doubt if I would be able to do it if I was in a similar situation.

But as well as individual forgiveness, whole communities need to be merciful to each other. They need to get beyond tribal hatred, going over old sores and nursing wrath to keep it warm. We try all sorts of ways to help people feel a wee bit more kindly toward the other side, let go some of the anger, cool it a bit, and listen to some of the pain of the other side.

At one point we began to have dialogue with the political wing of the paramilitary groups. We started with a fierce antagonism toward each other. It was very difficult to shake hands with these guys, the murderers of our people, and our opening meetings were angry meetings. We shouted at each other, we called each other names, but after a few weeks we ran out of steam. We carried on with difficulty and calmed down enough to start listening. You began to hear their stories and to wonder, "If I were in their shoes, would I not be a gunman?" And then hopefully they were saying, "If I were a Unionist, would I not be feeling it's right to defend my people?" Real dialogue that is of God can work a miracle by beginning to soften our hearts.

We used to begin those meetings with reading, "Mercy and peace have met together and have kissed each other in the street" (Psalm 85). We read that same psalm every time we met, and gradually it seemed to penetrate. God begins to soften you. Then you begin to realize that the other people are human, even though you still can't understand why they are leading a murderous campaign of political violence, which I firmly believe never was and never is justified. Nevertheless, you begin to see how people can get so angry and frustrated, and feel so disadvantaged by the powerful group, that their anger spills over into violence.

It's easy to demonize. The Roman Catholic paramilitaries would talk about the police with vehemence and hatred, and call them bastards. Of course, many of them had been beaten to a pulp by some of these policemen. They had been confined, tortured, and taunted, and how else would you expect them to regard the police? But I also met policemen who were fine

Christian men, doing the almost impossible job of trying to police this community, and doing it with great courage even though they were prime targets. You can write off a whole lot of people as "psychopaths" or whatever. Some may be, but they're not all demons. Many are good people.

Forgiveness is a process. You think you have forgiven people and you suddenly realize you are still carrying anger. Gerry, my Roman Catholic priest friend, tells a story about being in a pulpit in Clonard. The reading was that passage from Paul describing how God is in Christ reconciling the world, not holding our trespasses against us. Suddenly he realized that with the police, the army, the British regime, he was holding their sins against them. This was a shock for someone working for twenty years in peace and reconciliation.

It's a long process: beginning to listen, beginning to take on board the pains and sufferings of the other side, beginning to understand. It's a journey that needs continual work. Again and again you come back to prayer, back to scripture, back to your knees in confession, back to asking for help to go at it again.

You Can't Dine on Poison

Tom Hannon's Story

I am the director of the Cornerstone Community here on the Springfield Road in Belfast. Being director means that I answer the correspondence, wash the dishes, and put the garbage out. We have been here as a small ecumenical community since 1982. The Springfield Road forms the peace line in West Belfast. All in front of us is Roman Catholic, all behind is Protestant, and we are here in the middle. I like to think of us as a little parable of possibility because we are a group of Catholics and Protestants who have come together to live in community. Not all of us live in the house. I don't live here, although my wife thinks I do. I go home from time to time, watch television, and see if she has changed much.

We started as a prayer group in Clonard Monastery, praying, studying scripture, and exchanging ideas together, once every two weeks for about seven years, before we discerned we were being called to some sort of community life together. We opened the house in 1982.

The Troubles started here in 1969. I was involved in one or two cross-community projects in my home. In December that year our youngest son, aged three and a half, was diagnosed as having leukaemia. This meant we spent an awful lot of time in our local children's hospital where there were children with chronic ailments like cystic fibrosis, haemophilia, and spina bifida, and I was thinking to myself, "Is this not the trouble we should be tackling? Is there not enough natural hurt in this world without us bringing in the bullets and bombs and tensions and fighting and anger?" My boy died at seven and a half, and people gathered round and were very good to us.

In October 1975 my oldest daughter, Mary, was shot coming from the pictures not far from here. She was eighteen at the time. She's still in a wheelchair. That put us back into the whole hospital thing again. When they sent her to England for treatment, it meant trouble for us to find the money to go and visit. But at the textile-engineering factory where I was working, I was given an envelope with an airline ticket and about £20 to go and see her, and later another envelope with a ticket and money that I used to pay for Mary to come home.

The majority of people working in the factory were Protestants. We, a Catholic family, were helped through that trauma by Protestant friends, Protestant workmates. That's something we will never forget, and whenever people start talking in a sectarian fashion, I don't mind telling them that story. It brought me into the peace movement. I am not sure I wouldn't react violently in certain circumstances, but I am aware of the total uselessness of violence.

My daughter recovered and went to work in Switzerland as a laboratory technician. After she came back, she went to university and took her degree. When television interviewed her at the degree ceremony, she said, "I am not disabled, I just can't walk." She's now doing a doctorate, and a year ago she got married and, at forty-one, produced her first baby.

People used to ask me if they got the fellas that shot her. It was obviously a Loyalist shooting. When you talk about forgiveness, I can honestly say that, if the men responsible had been in the hospital that night, I would not have had a word to say to them. But you can't dine on poison or you poison yourself. Still, we have to recognize that sometimes people have nothing else to hold on to but the hurt. Giving it up means asking, "Who am I other than my pain?"' That's an awful situation to be in.

One of the things we have done here in Cornerstone is to visit families across the divide who have been bereaved for whatever reason, whether they were Loyalist paramilitaries or security forces or Republican paramilitaries. Sam Burch, a Methodist minister, started this visiting across the lines with Fr. Gerry, the local Catholic priest.

There was a young man shot not too far from here, a member of the Ulster Defence Regiment, a regiment of the British army. He was shot dead by the IRA. Gerry rang up Sam and said, "Look, I would like to go and visit the family." Gerry, a Roman Catholic priest, was going to cross the Shankill Road, and Sam was apprehensive. However, the two of them went along. Guys were standing round the door, and the young widow was too distraught to talk, but they went next door to the young man's parents' house and met the mother. Gerry had brought with him a little wooden carved head of the Christ with the crown of thorns. Sam introduced him and said why they had come, and Gerry offered to pray with them. The mother started to cry and Gerry started to weep, and the tears fell on the little woodcut so it looked as though Christ was crying for his people.

Another story. Members of the Cornerstone Community attend the funerals. I remember visiting a little house where the daughter, aged thirteen, had been killed in a bombing. The family had gone to the funeral, but there was a lady giving out tea and sandwiches as we do here, and we were made welcome. A little girl was sitting in the narrow room and crying her eyes out. She was a Catholic who had been on holiday with the Protestant girl who had been killed — a cross-community holiday in the United States — and she had come to say farewell to her friend. Sometimes healing comes from feeling the hurt of the other side.

A final story. When a man was shot one afternoon after attending his son's birthday party, we went down to the house and talked to people, telling them who we were and how sorry we were and suggesting that, if it was appropriate, we would pray with them. We also suggested that one month later there could be a little service in their home. We asked his widow up to Cornerstone one day to talk about it. She sat between us at the window. While we were talking, there was a ring at the door-bell. Two children were there, and they asked for a goldfish bowl. "What do you want with a goldfish bowl?" I asked. They looked at me rather pityingly and said, "For a goldfish." The logic was inescapable. I rummaged around and found an old casserole dish and gave it to them.

There we were in a highly sensitive meeting, trying to help this woman through her trauma, and we were also helping a couple of kids with a goldfish bowl. It was a sign that even in the midst of bombs and bullets, goldfish are important. It seemed like a vindication to us that we are getting something right.

Living in the Middle

Shelagh Livingstone's Story

I am a member of Cornerstone Community, a community of reconciliation in West Belfast. I used to be a teacher and then moved into community work. Over a period of about eleven years I visited inside the Maze Prison as a member of the board of visitors who met many of the prisoners, particularly those from a paramilitary background but also ordinary prisoners.

I was trying to explore as a Christian what it means to love my neighbour and to love my enemy. This was in the 1970s when the Troubles were at their height, and when it seemed to me, as a Protestant living in Belfast, that my enemy was primarily the IRA and the Provisional IRA. Visiting at the Maze Prison turned a lot of my presuppositions upside down. I found there not the ruthless, dedicated criminals that the newspapers told me I would find, but ordinary, concerned people who cared about me and my welfare, and about the welfare of their own community. They were involved in what they called fighting, and the newspapers called terrorism, because they saw this as the only way open to them to improve the situation they were living in. Some of them became very close friends of mine.

For me, this touches very closely on notions of forgiveness. I had to ask, Do I have anything to forgive? How does forgiveness relate to loving my enemy? I had to review all my presuppositions about the society in which I lived, including the assumptions that those in authority are usually right, usually honest. All those assumptions went out the window. I also struggled with the idea of scapegoating. Reconciliation, scapegoating, forgiveness, loving of neighbour and enemy are all very closely associated in my mind and experience.

During the 1970s there were gangs opeating in our community. I was terrified to walk home from work at night because of them. Some gang members were tried and convicted of murder. When they came to trial, I realized that I knew one of them by sight. I always found it impossible to come to terms with them in my own mind, because they came from my own community.

No matter how hard I tried, I couldn't really believe they were capable of change, and I couldn't bring myself to forgive them. But I knew somewhere inside me that I was going to have to face up to this one, because my Christian understanding was that change was possible for everybody.

Then I heard that one of them had had a sort of Pauline Damascus road experience. Cynically, I thought he had gone through the motions to get an early release date. He eventually served twenty-two years. I had met him when he first came into jail, but when I met him again, he was utterly transformed by the love of Christ. That was a very humbling experience for me. It demonstrated in a new way what forgiveness is — it is always there in the heart of God.

I have also had to wrestle with the question, Do I have a right to forgive a man for murdering somebody else? At some level, obviously, I don't have that right. But at another level we have to be prepared to be forgiving toward people, no matter who they are and what they do. The people I, as a Protestant, find most difficult to forgive are the Loyalist paramilitaries. Catholic members of our community often find the Republican people are the most difficult to forgive.

I've bought a house in the area and continue to live in between the separated communities. There are many other people who have lived through the Troubles and do not want to go on living in this segregated way. They have recognized the need for safety for their families and are looking for opportunities to meet the other side and bring their children up in a different way. So I'm not alone. Cornerstone is on the peace line, demonstrating to people in the area this possibility of living together, and many people have welcomed it.

Of course, many people have moved out, but some, particularly senior citizens, have lived here for many, many years. They knew each other but hadn't had opportunities to meet for a long time because all the shops were closed or demolished, there were no eating places, and the churches were places where they went separately. So we started a senior citizens' lunch club down in the Methodist church once a week. People came from both sides of the community, kept on coming, and wanted more. One of the Catholic men actually said to me after the lunch club had been going for about five years, "Shelagh, the best thing that ever happened on this road since the Troubles began was this lunch club." A group of senior citizens have a kind of stability that any community needs. When you see senior citizens happily meeting together week by week, and walking down the road talking together, it's like a parable.

At the lunch club itself the conversation tends to be fairly light and social, but some have been to the Corrymeela Community for residential experiences and have shared stories at a deeper level. Other things happen too. One of the men suddenly didn't come one week. When I met him later, he explained that he had been stopped while walking up the road after mass by two men who asked if he was a member of the lunch club. They said, "Don't you be coming back here again, or we'll see to it that you don't." He knew this was a death threat. So he stayed away for two weeks and then said, "I'm not going to be intimidated in this way, I'm coming back again."

For me, part of learning to forgive is in the experience of not being safe in my own city. All the places that I love in Northern Ireland — places where people went for picnics or lovely holidays — have become a litany of the dead. But recognizing the situation in which young people grow up has helped me to come to terms with this sad fact. Since I come from a fairly middle-class background, it wasn't until I started working on the Shankill that I saw the appalling living conditions of people in the early seventies — two-roomed houses with a toilet out in the backyard and thirteen living there, lack of opportunities in jobs, terrible social injustices.

Joining an army gave young men status and something worthwhile to do and a sense of importance within themselves. A friend of mine, a Catholic, told the story of her eldest son joining the British army in June of 1969. He was posted back here and was on a vehicle checkpoint. In a car they were checking out someone who was his best friend from school. This friend had joined the IRA. He said to his mother, "Mum, if I hadn't joined the British army in June 1969, by August I would have joined the IRA."

I have tried putting the blame on all sorts of people, but in the end it doesn't work. In my head I know that blaming is a useless operation, but in the heart it is still active. Little things keep bringing it up. Some of my anger has been directed against the security forces, because I saw in West Belfast some of the horrendous things they did. There was a wee boy who lived across the road from me, aged about five. A foot patrol was going along the road, and he padded along beside a soldier, pointed at his gun, and said, "What's that?" The soldier said, "It's a gun."' The boy asked, "What's it for?" The soldier replied, "For shooting Taigs" (Catholics). I was so angry when I heard about it, and I was helpless to do anything. Suddenly I could understand the frustration of a whole community in that kind of situation. So how do you set about forgiving the security forces?

I think sheer bloody-mindedness keeps me going. So does Christian faith. The excitement of exploring a Christian faith calls you to work on the edges and meet wonderful people. A lot of affirmation comes from that.

Forgiveness Is So Difficult

Angela Donnelly's Story

I am an outreach worker at the Wave Centre in Belfast, and I visit families that have been bereaved or traumatized by the Troubles. I have a particular understanding of this because in 1981, my brother was abducted, and for three years we didn't know what had happened to him. In 1984 his body was recovered in a bog in Dundalk, just by accident. He was a member of the IRA, though we didn't know that at the time.

Because of the stigma attached to someone who is a terrorist, we grieved in total isolation. It was difficult to talk about him or even acknowledge that he had been murdered. Only since I became a member of Wave, about four years ago, have I actually ever mentioned the word murder. But with the acknowledgement came the reality, and I had to deal with things. I still receive counselling, which helps me greatly in the work that I do. A relationship needs to be built up when we go into people's homes, and somewhere along the line people will ask, "Have you had any involvement in the Troubles yourself? Has anyone died in your own family?" There's a total change of atmosphere when we outreach workers can say Yes and share our own experiences. There's an immediate empathy that just isn't there when someone hasn't been directly affected.

I'm amazed at how many families deal with the tragedies — particularly women whose husbands have been murdered — and they struggle on, raising their families. In my own family we didn't talk about my brother, even when his body was recovered. To this day not one of us nine children knows the full story of what happened. To ask questions would always upset my mother and make my father very angry. I found out my own way by going to the libraries and looking up anything on terrorism in Northern Ireland, and I found a book that had a section about him. I had wondered about him when we were growing up, because he was immature and into slogans and wanting to be "a big fella," but he had no idea of the history of Ireland. Sometimes he would be picked up by the police, which wasn't uncommon for young men.

He disappeared on two occasions for a week, apparently lifted by the IRA. They used to do horrible things like put a hood over his head and leave him naked and beat him, before they released him. But equally he would tell stories about how the police would strip him and duck his head in cold water. Were these stories of someone who wanted to be the "big fella," or was this really happening to him? When his body was recovered, I felt a huge amount of guilt — if I had believed him, would things have been different? He was twenty-seven, his first wife had died, and his new wife was pregnant. One morning, after a New Year's party, he went out to get milk and potatoes. He never came back.

The people who murdered my brother have never been caught. I don't know if I could ever forgive them for shooting him in cold blood. But that doesn't stop me doing the work that I do, and it doesn't stop me understanding that, when we talk about victims in Northern Ireland, there's always the question, Who is the real victim? To an extent we are all victims. But I have difficulty with forgiveness. Possibly the time might come when I could sit down with whoever shot him and see from their point of view. I also recognize that I don't know if my brother did the same thing to someone else. I don't know whether I could forgive him. He was in the IRA. I don't want to know any more because I am ashamed that he was in a paramilitary organization. I don't mourn for a terrorist. I mourn for my brother.

In my work I find that people move in their own time. The relief of just saying what has actually happened, with nobody sitting over you in judgement, is tremendous; but to actually sit with people and talk about the emotional impact of it, will always upset me. Things have unfolded for me when I've been ready. Having gone into counselling, and shared with other people, has helped to dissolve the emotional pain, and I feel in time it will just be in me, but it won't be a block that is stuck in my chest or my stomach.

Tolerance comes from listening to someone else totally opposite. My experience could be locked into the kind of Catholic thinking that says, "If it weren't for how Protestants treated Catholics in the first place, if there had been better housing and good jobs, then there wouldn't have been violence in the first place." But my father was a Protestant who turned Catholic to marry a Catholic, as you had to in those days, so I have Protestant relatives. When I got to the point that I could tell my whole story to people who could understand the emotional impact, the next step was to listen to someone who was a Loyalist and find that they were talking exactly the way I was talking. The tears are the same, the pain is the same. It's like symmetry in a mirror. You come together in the pain.

There is something bigger and greater than I that is given the name God. God isn't something that is up in my head anymore. Religion isn't ritual anymore. It's in me, and I get great strength from it.

Personal Responsibility

Hugh Megarry's Story

In 1969 I was shot three times in one day. The third time I was shot in the face and chest, which left me blind. In hospital they told me there wasn't much hope for my sight. But I was quite lucky. I got a social worker in hospital who was semi-retired, but she had been a specialist worker for the blind. Since I was asking the time repeatedly, she brought me a big alarm clock with bells, no face, saying, "Don't be asking the time again." That sort of kick-started me to realize I could have some semblance of independence, and I started learning Braille within two weeks of losing my sight. Then I went to a rehabilitation centre for the blind in Torquay, came back, did a lot of training in engineering, and was unemployed for about three years.

During those three years I came very close to a breakdown on a number of occasions, through lack of work, lack of dignity, all that. But I did get a job eventually in an engineering factory, and worked there for years and became involved in organizations for and of the blind. Then I got into mainstream community work, trying to improve things for myself and people like me. I got a job with Northern Ireland Community Enterprises, working with a group of people who had become disabled because of the Troubles. I left after about three years, worked voluntarily on the Shankill for a further year, and then got a job with Belfast City Council, where I have been for over sixteen years. I move about to different community centres. At present I am doing a course, a diploma in Youth Work, at university.

People ask me if I hate Catholics. But it wasn't a quarter of a million people with their finger on the trigger that day; it was an individual. I can't blame all Catholics for that. I have to blame the individual and the situation — the situation we have all found ourselves in here since the late sixties. As teenagers it was a big laugh to beat up on the other side — fun — and there is still an element of that. I can see it in fourteen- and fifteen-year-olds in the area now. The two different groups meet and say they're going to have a battle on Friday night, and yet other times in the week they're quite friendly. This doesn't happen to everyone — don't get me wrong.

But I know of other people on both sides who have lost family, and they find it very difficult to forgive either the individual or the community. I think the whole peace process neglected victims. For instance, from the Unionist perspective, you see Catholic politicians shoving peace down your throat every day, and you know that some of them standing on that platform are directly responsible for deaths. And Catholics see Unionist politicians pushing for peace, who have been directly responsible for deaths. There needs to be some sort of healing process, and that hasn't been put in place.

There are different categories of victims. Someone now in prison, who had the choice, who took a gun in his hand and put a finger on the trigger, is different from the person he shot who didn't have a gun. I don't say that as someone who has clean hands. In 1969 I was as involved in the rioting as anybody else. I was stone throwing; I was petrol bombing — the lot. So I am a perpetrator as well as a victim.

There are a lot of different ways that people cope with loss and trying to forgive. Some people can't find it in their hearts to forgive openly and honestly. I think there are other people who are genuinely trying to take the Christian approach to things and want to forgive, but they're torn apart inside because they still have the hatred there and they think it's wrong. Most people don't understand that they're not wrong. It's only human to hate and want revenge; and to get through that process, you need a lot of support. Others can forgive. I think Gordon Wilson, a man from Enniskillen who lay in the rubble with his daughter who had just been killed, genuinely meant it when he said he forgave the perpetrators. It took me a long time to come to terms with that because I was saying, "Your daughter died there with you, and you're saying you forgive!" But at the end of the day I suppose that's the only way we are going to get any peace.

I'm involved in a project about restorative justice in which we are trying to encourage paramilitary organizations to walk away from beatings. It was something I had to work out for myself. A child was killed by a stolen car that was returning from a paramilitary beating. That child was in the same class as my grandson. For about two months I really had to think this through — Should I still be involved in alternatives, or are paramilitaries making fools of us? I realized that walking away from the problem wasn't helping the situation, and that I am part of the problem. I am part of the community. When you see paramilitary beatings, you don't say, "That was ridiculous." You say, "I wonder what he did?" On occasion I have said to myself, "Well, a good bloody beating will do him the world of good." So because I have said that, I understand that, in a way, I too am responsible for that child's death.

I've been involved in cross-community work for fifteen years, and I still have a lot of prejudices. I have to accept that I have the prejudices and that I have to work through them. Being prejudiced doesn't stop you being able to do the work. It's being aware that you are prejudiced that is important. It's being aware that some of the things you say are offensive.

People need to be made aware. I remember working with a group of kids around Belfast together with a girl from a Catholic community centre. Then came the Shankill bombings. Afterwards, we met again with the kids from the two groups, and we realized that two kids from each side had had relatives killed. That was extremely difficult to work through, and the sessions became much more intense. We can recognize mutual prejudice, and we can try to work it through, but in the end we know it's never going to be a perfect world.

Political correctness has gone over the top. My disability would be referred to as visually impaired, visually challenged. I'm blind — that's it! I'm blind. I used to be able to get up on a Saturday morning, put a few sandwiches and a flask in a haversack, and go out to the country. There was a coppice just outside Bally Clare that I always remember around September or October when all the leaves were in colour and so beautiful, and there were always woodcock in it. That's the main thing I feel angry about. I can't go out and appreciate the countryside. I loved the solitude, but now there always has to be someone around.

I suppose I'm lucky that I have the visual memories, but that also sharpens the loss. Belfast can look a grimy, dull city, but there is nowhere in Belfast that you can't look up at the mountains. It's a marvellous place to live, with very friendly people when they're not killing each other.

It's a
Costly Thing to Do

Martie Rafferty's Story

I used to work for a voluntary project called Kairos that started in 1997. For the fourteen years before that, I spent time working in the prisons with political prisoners, ex-prisoners, and their families. I still work in the community now with ex-prisoners, and also with victims of paramilitary violence.

I am a Quaker, and I often think I was brought into this work by God because I needed to learn something. The Quakers appealed to me because of their pacifism, and in my experience the other churches didn't proclaim justice centrally. As a young community worker out in the streets of Belfast, I saw the damage being done by the paramilitaries and the young people being led into them, and I felt the paramilitaries were totally wrong. Then when people started talking about the things that were happening to the paramilitaries in interrogation centres and prisons, I can remember saying that, whatever they got, they deserved. If you live by the gun you die by it, and that's the choice you make. I had absolutely no sympathy. And I was quite content that a Christian pacifism was what Jesus wanted and that these people were totally off the rails.

Then I formally became a member of the Society of Friends.

One morning at the end of the meeting, it was announced that one of the Elders had started up a visiting centre at the prison. We had never had big prisons before. So when they opened up Long Kesh — as it then was, The Maze now — the system couldn't cope. It was an emergency situation, and people were being rounded up without trial and interned. There were no visiting systems in place. The families would come up in busloads from Belfast, and stand out in the rain while somebody tried to figure out who was visiting who and how to arrange it. It was a real flashpoint, and actual violence did break out from time to time.

The Quakers set up a centre to shelter the families. One of the women said she needed volunteers to come and make tea. She spoke quite movingly and said, "No matter what you may think of the prisoners, their families are innocent." I couldn't ignore the message. I really didn't want to do it, but I felt I had to. So I went. It was only for a half day a week, and I thought, "This is just for the families; I really don't care what happens to the prisoners." Of course, once I was there and came to know the families, I cared about them very much, and I found myself going a couple of days a week. But soon they needed people full-time to help with childcare and to give advice and counselling. So the organizer and I decided that we would cover it full-time.

The families would bring you their concerns, and gradually I realized that this prisoner — this terrorist — was actually somebody's son or somebody's husband or somebody's daddy. The children would come up crying for their daddy. Of course, you then got to see that nobody is one-dimensional. These terrorists are actually people who are loved and missed. Your image of them changed. They weren't just nameless, murdering terrorists anymore.

Eventually we went into the prison to conduct seminars for the prisoners, and in conjunction with many other groups we managed to change prison policy and get an emphasis on the family, by showing how important it was to maintain family life. Any study done would show that the stronger the family link, the less chance there is of recidivism and re-offending. So even cynical, money-effective terms, it makes sense. We managed to transform the whole visiting procedure. There are excellent visiting facilities up there now, with childcare and everything inside the jail and a really good environment.

Over fourteen years you become very close to people. The average sentence there is twelve to sixteen years, so the same people would come up to the centre the same day every week for years. You got to know people, and saw the children grow up and parents get old and ill, and you saw how that affected prisoners. They had the same concerns about families as we do. You discovered the full range of human emotion there, no matter what the press was saying about evil people. The deeds they had done were awful, but they were done by people who had the full range of capacity and emotion that we all do. I once heard a man say, "I can't imagine how I did it. I feel I was a different person then. I know it was me, and I'm still carrying it, but I now wonder how I ever got to that point." I felt that I was brought in there to learn that Christianity is more than pacifism.

I never checked up prisoners' records. I never asked the person who they were or what they'd done. We just started from two people meeting each day. That was the only way I could handle it. The prisoners knew I was a Quaker who didn't believe in violence for any reason, and they knew I respected them anyway, and they did the same with me. On that basis we could move closer together.

A lot of people outside, including my family, used to get annoyed with me, as though I was somehow aiding and abetting terrorism. There was one particular bombing in Enniskillen that killed a lot of people at a memorial service, and it shocked and outraged the community. It was one of the attacks that had tremendous impact. People phoned and yelled at me as though it was my fault. I thought, "Well, one thing I can be very sure of is that the people I am actually working with didn't do it, because they are all in jail."

I try to remember and understand the gospel message about unconditional love. It's not talking about loving people only if they change. I know that, especially here in Northern Ireland, we think, "First you repent, and then we can forgive you." But that's not what the gospel message is. I think you love people whether they repent or not, and the love itself very often brings about the repentance. I have actually seen it work.

No matter what we have done, there is a spiritual spark in everyone, and also the capacity for evil. I think it is our Christian duty to seek the spiritual spark and recognize it when it shines out. When I was talking to somebody in prison, I really tried to see the human being, and I found this actually allowed the spark to grow in the person. To me it has made the gospel message very clear — you love people just as they are.

I got a good deal of support from my own Quaker community, and the feedback from the prisoners and their families taught me so much. I learned a lot about loyalty to families and to principles, and about courage and humour. But it was often the prison staff who made the work difficult, what with verbal abuse, innuendo, lies, and even accusations of colluding with the IRA. I had a close line of contact with the Northern Ireland office, and could report on what I'd seen, and the prison staff didn't like that. One person even said, "We cannot have a free spirit running around here." Lies especially could have been very dangerous. The prisoners and their families tried to protect me as much as they could.

Eventually I moved back to working in the wider community. There I met with some of the released prisoners and helped set up some of the self-help centres. But I saw that, when the ceasefires were declared, instead of celebration there was an upsurge of anger and resentment in the community. It was almost as if everything that people had been keeping the lid on for all those years was given permission to come out, and I realized two things. One is that ceasefires and peace agreements were not going to get rid of the anger, fear, and resentment. Structures needed to be put in place to proactively begin a healing process. Secondly, I realized that the group I had been working with in the prisons — the paramilitary prisoners from both Loyalist and Republican traditions, and their families — were very quickly being made the scapegoats for the whole thirty years. Nobody ever looked at what anybody else had contributed to the pain, by things they had done or by their attitudes.

So I felt very angry. Like everyone else, I carry my own baggage of anger and resentment. And I began to think, "There is so much work to be done out in the community. Maybe I would be more use there than in the prisons." So in 1997 I started working with groups like Wave and Survivors of Trauma, and I heard the awful raw pain of those who had been injured or bereaved by the men that I was so committed to. For instance, I listened to someone whose son was taken away and killed, or disappeared, and she couldn't find the body. But these people were not the most vociferous in blaming the paramilitaries.

In many ways, the people who had been worst hurt were more generous than the politicians and the population at large — the respectable, middle-class, law-abiding citizens who never got involved in anything. They were the ones who were most judgemental and vindictive. My vision is that somehow we can eventually reach that population, but it will be difficult because they don't know that there is anything wrong in their attitudes.

It's just not a black and white world. The world isn't full of victims and perpetrators. It's full of people who belong in both categories simultaneously. In fact, I suspect there is a victim and a perpetrator within each of us. You have to accept that you are not changing the world, and it came to me that it's not my responsibility to change the world. Fr. Gerry Reynolds once said, "When you actually think you are being led by God and are trying to witness to the love of God, success doesn't come into it. Failure is only a problem if success is the goal. The real goal is witnessing. If you genuinely witness the gospel in your life, you can't fail, because you are not doing it to change everybody you meet; you are doing it to live out your understanding of the gospel." I think the example of Jesus helps because, What did he do? Got himself crucified! Anyone who wants to follow him will be crucified in some way or other. You will feel lonely and isolated and rejected at times, but that is what witnessing to the way of Jesus is.

I have never considered that anything I was doing was on the theme of reconciliation. To me that was a lovely by-product of the work. For instance, I tried to convince people from both sides that they'd be more likely to get grants to help re-establish themselves in the community if they worked together; then the government and other funders would be less likely to suspect them of wanting to get money to hand on to their paramilitary organizations.

We started a program that we learned from Michael Apsley and his Healing of Memories program in South Africa. It's about giving people a safe place to bring their pain. We've had ex-prisoners, both Loyalist and Republican, and people whose relatives were killed by those organizations, all listening to one another. Some of the relatives felt they were betraying the memories of their loved ones just by sitting and engaging with these people. Some of the prisoners were scared stiff at being face to face with the victims. But it worked because there was just a safe place for people to come together.

I believe that if you give safety and respect love, then no matter what story they are telling, you can see normal human beings who have God in them.

Reflection

Forgiveness in Northern Ireland?

Sooner or later we have to consider the word "forgive" itself. A dictionary will produce meanings such as pardon, overlook, remit (a debt), cease to bear anger or resentment, let go, absolve, show mercy. But we need more than a word to capture the experience of forgiveness. So I turn to the image that lies at the heart of Western Christian culture — the cross.

Christians believe that, in the person of Jesus, we meet one who is fully human and fully God — God approachable. On Calvary our inhumanity to each other is fully revealed for what it is. The cross was a dreadful, barbaric institution of torture and death for those who had fallen foul of the Roman empire. More than that, the cross reveals our response to the goodness, holiness, and love of God — rejection, hatred, and murder. God responded, not by annihilating his failed creation, but by giving back to men and women the result of their sin, transformed now into a sign of forgiveness and hope through the resurrection of Jesus. His followers ever since have seen the figure on the cross as offering forgiveness, refusing to return evil for evil, and so opening the way to reconciliation with God and each other.

In the risen Christ, God gives humanity not merely a future it had no right to expect, but a future with hope.... It frees the forgiven to take action on behalf of others. To be thus forgiven is to be both empowered and enjoined to forgive each other. Forgiveness is therefore at the heart of the Christian community.[1]

But the cross is not just a symbol of transformation and hope; it also shows what is required in any act of forgiveness. Gabriel Daly quotes a passage from Dag Hammarskjold, who wrote, "Forgiveness breaks the chain of causality because he who forgives you — out of love — takes upon himself the consequences of what you have done. Forgiveness, therefore, always entails sacrifice."[2]

As many in Northern Ireland have found in their own struggles, such sacrifice involves not only conquering all the natural emotions of anger, disgust, and fear in the face of particular acts of violence, but also abandoning the temptation to hold onto these feelings as a kind of solace. Such sacrifice also means abandoning the stances where I am wholly right and you are wholly wrong. Time and time again I was deeply impressed by the way people refused the sharp distinctions between perpetrator and victim as they struggled to emerge from their own history of suffering.

---

1 Gabriel Daly, Alan D. Falconer, and Joseph Liechty, eds., *Reconciling Memories* (Dublin: Columba Press, 1998), pp. 207f.
2 *Reconciling Memories*, p. 203.

Since forgiveness lies at the heart of the gospel, sectarian violence between communities with Christian foundations is an irony. Not surprisingly then, I found anger among some of the ex-prisoners, and among some of the younger people in Belfast, at the failure of the churches to be more reconciling communities and less trapped in the divisions of the province. I was warned early in my visit that the meaning of the word forgiveness depended on the community you came from. Each operated on the basis of complicated stereotypes.

The Roman Catholic Church could be seen as allowing for human failure during the slow formation of a Christian, especially by providing sacramental confession and forgiveness. However, being a fairly hierarchical church, it could also be viewed from the outside as emphasizing disproportionately the church's authority to declare God's mind and forgiveness. Sacramental confession and forgiveness may or may not help the penitent, depending on the depth of confession and the recognition of the reality of sin. But the church could be perceived as doling out forgiveness in return for superficial repentance, making no real difference to behaviour.

Some Protestant churches could be seen as rejecting any human mediation of forgiveness, with the consequence of privatizing confession and forgiveness altogether. Their emphasis on being a converted community, called out of a sinful world, could be seen by outsiders as leading to harsh demands for good behaviour in an atmosphere of judgementalism. You are a sinner. You must repent. You have to earn forgiveness. You might be forgiven in this world, but more likely in the next.

I am trying to convey the understanding of people brought up in these traditions as they were described to me. The third understanding of forgiveness — which many from both communities shared with me — was a discovery of the unconditional love of God, which does not condone the sin but never rejects the sinner. God longs for us to turn from sinful behaviour and toward a love that brings us into life in all its fullness. Unconditional love seeks to draw out repentance rather than require it first. Some of those who had lost loved ones made the notable and essential step of recognizing that they too carried some responsibility for the way things were by assenting to the division in the community. Growing through their own suffering, escaping from the traps of blame and revenge, they have been led to help others, victims and perpetrators, to be released into growth as well.

It was equally notable how many were also seeking creative ways of turning away from a violent past when they came out of prison. Some of them were already clear about God's love and forgiveness of them. The repentance was released by the forgiveness and took the form of practical and courageous action — courageous because ex-prisoners had to face the possibility that their own communities might reject them for seeking ways to heal the divisions.

Who is in a position to forgive whom? Few families of victims will ever discover the names of the individuals who committed acts of violence. They seek first to discover what happened. The challenge then is to be released from a rage that desires revenge, and to emerge into an attitude of forgiveness toward the unknown perpetrators. They may have to go through this process every day for many years. It can be just as difficult when the identity of the perpetrators is suspected but not proved from lack of evidence. For those who still do not know what happened, or still have not recovered a body so that grieving may be released, the process of moving beyond a place where things cannot be named, the process of grieving and forgiving, is even more difficult. It is equally difficult for those who have perpetrated violence to receive forgiveness, either because they do not know their victims, or because they do not know whether the families would be prepared to meet them, let alone forgive them.

Hugh emphasized the importance of personal responsibility. He recognized his own involvement in the early years building up to the violent confrontation, and he turned from that. "My hands are not clean.... I am a perpetrator as well as a victim." He could also recognize that it was only one person who pulled the trigger, not the whole Catholic community. His mother struggled to forgive the person for blinding her son. Hugh is not sure where he is in the process of forgiving, but meanwhile he tries to turn other young people away from the paths of bigotry and violence.

Shelagh suffered indirectly from the activities of the gangs — the fear of violence prevented her from walking directly home in the evening. They claimed to be acting on her behalf as a Protestant. She rejected this claim completely, but she felt that her community was tarnished by their claim (as did many Catholics by the corresponding claims and activities of the IRA). As Angela showed, families who discover that one of their members has joined the paramilitary can find it difficult to come to terms with what he might or might not have done. Forgiveness is not just a matter of the offended forgiving the offender. There is also a community dimension, though it is far less clear how one community can forgive another community.

The cost to those who stay in the middle, vulnerable to both sides, respecting without necessarily agreeing with either, has been enormous. It has meant not denying the evil of appalling acts, while attempting to see the human behind the label and God within the human. Believing that God's forgiveness comes first has led to a crucifying cost of witnessing to the love of God, which neither condones nor denies but looks beyond. Sectarian violence hides from public gaze those people who try to live out the Christian gospel.

The role of the state

When I asked whether it was possible to talk about communities forgiving each other, the consensus seemed to be that forgiveness has to begin with individuals, so that communities grow into a new way of regarding each other with respect and without fear or rancour. However, it is worth remembering that what the state does has profound effects on the way people can relate.

In 1998 the British government met with political parties from across the spectrum in Northern Ireland, and on Good Friday of that year they came to an agreement. It resulted in a ceasefire from the paramilitaries, began the staged withdrawal of the British armed forces, put into place the goal of reducing arms, and set up the structure for a local government for the province. I was in Belfast in 1999, a year later. There is no doubt in my mind that the agreement, flawed as it might be, released a great deal of energy and hope among many people there. I saw no soldiers on the streets of Belfast, and not many police either.

Communities had begun breathing once again. Cross-community ventures could work more easily, though of course there was still a great deal of trepidation, and the paramilitary groups had not lost their power in some areas. The question was whether politicians and political parties would resist the demagoguery of the past and start looking at how to govern the province for everyone, not just their own people. There is a long way to go yet.

The Good Friday agreement did not just release hope. After the ceasefire, there were arguments as to what the agreement meant, especially about the decommissioning of weapons and the release of prisoners, and a great deal of anger also erupted. After so many years of silence, people felt more able to talk in public about their past painful experiences. The BBC in Northern Ireland ran a story each day for many months. Feelings of anger and grief and frustration came to the surface as people asked, "What has all this suffering achieved?" Neutral parties have been called in to oversee the decommissioning, but none of the states directly involved is neutral and able to provide an environment in which people can grow through and away from the past.

The British and Irish governments have both been deeply involved in the Troubles of the past. The challenge remains: Can all the parties involved — the United Kingdom, the Republic of Ireland, the political parties of Northern Ireland, the paramilitaries — grow sufficiently, and bring their constituencies with them, to create a working structure in which all the people can face the future creatively?

Can communities let go of the self-justifying stances of the past, the responses of blame, the defining of identity by creating enemies to resist? Can they discover a common history together and absorb the hurt that each has inflicted by attitude and action on the other? Some in Northern Ireland turned for inspiration to South Africa, where another extraordinary and fascinating exploration was taking place.

Community Forgiveness

Truth and Reconciliation in South Africa

Truth and Reconciliation in South Africa

In 1964 the peaceful campaign for racial justice led by the Rev. Martin Luther King in the USA was commanding headlines. From our home in Canada we had been watching with hope as American society struggled to emerge from its racist past. So when the opportunity came to teach in another part of the world, we went to Basutoland (now Lesotho), a small country in the mountains, completely surrounded by South Africa.

We joined a fledgling campus of the new university, where over twenty nationalities were represented, including students and staff from South Africa. We were already aware of apartheid in South Africa — the official policy that kept races apart and ensured that the white minority retained political, economic, and military control over the black majority. We wanted to experience what it was like without having to live under it. South Africa is a beautiful country, graced with some extraordinary people. But the tensions were already increasing after the Sharpeville massacres of 1960, when police fired into an unarmed crowd of black people who had gathered to protest against the increasingly harsh laws of discrimination. Over thirty people died that day. Appalled at the racial divisions and the oppression driven by the intransigent white leadership, we could see no future for the country but an eventual bloody civil war.

By the late 1980s international pressure through sanctions was taking its toll, and internal violence was increasing as the strength of groups such as the African National Congress (ANC) grew. Then on 2 February 1990 South African President F.W. de Klerk announced to an astonished world the unbanning of political organizations that had been proscribed since 1960. A week later Nelson Mandela, who had been in prison for twenty-five years as one of the leaders of the ANC, was released. Years of hard political bargaining followed to establish an interim constitution and prepare for the first elections to include black people. The intention of the interim constitution was to construct a society based on

> the recognition of human rights, democracy, and peaceful co-existence, and development of opportunities for all South Africans, irrespective of colour, race, class, belief or sex.... The bitter legacy of the past can now be addressed on the basis that there is a need for understanding but not for vengeance, a need for reparation but not for retaliation, a need for *ubuntu* [see explanation below, p. 119] but not for victimization. In order to advance such reconciliation and reconstruction, amnesty shall be granted in respect of acts, omissions, and offences associated with political objectives and committed in the course of the conflicts of the past.[1]

---

1 "Postscript to the Interim Constitution," in Desmond Tutu, *No Future Without Forgiveness: A Personal Overview of South Africa's Truth and Reconciliation Commission* (London: Rider & Co., 1999), pp. 45–46.

The postscript became the constitutional foundation of the Truth and Reconciliation Commission (TRC) set up by the new government in 1995. After much public consultation, seventeen commissioners representing the wide diversity of South African life were chosen by Nelson Mandela (then president), and the commission was to be chaired by Desmond Tutu, the Anglican Archbishop of Capetown. The TRC had three committees dealing with human rights violations, amnesty, and reparations and rehabilitation. The peaceful transition was an extraordinary achievement, requiring not just the courage of political leaders but also the moral stature of people like Nelson Mandela and Desmond Tutu. But they could not have done it without the labour, suffering, and magnanimity of spirit of so many others who had suffered so much.

Human rights violations

The Human Rights Violations Committee gave voice to the experiences of victims, witnesses, and perpetrators from all sides of the conflict that had occurred within or outside the country between 1 March 1960 (including Sharpeville) and 10 May 1994 (the inauguration of Nelson Mandela as president). By the end of the commission's lifespan, over 21,000 people had come forward — men and women, old and young — to relate their stories of some 38,000 gross violations of human rights. Nine out of ten were black, most were women, and the majority related stories on behalf of dead men to whom they were related.

The commission employed people to take their statements in their own language, through interpreters if necessary (there are eleven major languages in South Africa), and they employed others to offer counselling if asked. No one has any doubt that there are many more stories that never came to the commission. For each of the more than 21,000 people making submissions, the TRC was asked to recommend whether the individual should receive reparations and/or whether further investigations should follow.

Amnesty

The Amnesty Committee was given the judicial power to grant amnesty following amnesty applications and perpetrators' confessions. There were specific conditions: the application had to be registered before 30 September 1997; the act of violence must have occurred between 1 March 1960 and 10 May 1994; full disclosure of all relevant facts had to be made for acts of violence ordered by, or on behalf of, a political organization such as the apartheid state, its former, partly self-governing black areas called Bantustans, or a recognized liberation movement such as the African National Congress or the Pan Africanist Congress.

Victims had the right to oppose the application by showing that the conditions were not met, but they could not veto the amnesty. No remorse was required for amnesty, though many did express it. The vast majority of these applications were refused because they did not meet the conditions. Those who were granted amnesty were then immune from prosecution in a criminal or civil court. In other words, instead of relying on retribution, which is the form that justice often takes, the commission chose a broader form of justice by encouraging truth to be spoken.

Reparation

The Reparation and Rehabilitation Committee did not hold public hearings but received a huge number of applications from individuals who themselves, or whose families, had suffered gross violations of human rights. The committee was still struggling to get through its work when I was there in June 1999. They could only make recommendations to the government, but they tried to facilitate reparations wherever possible. It remains with the government to decide what final actions should be taken, and it is clear to many in South Africa that unless the grievances are met in some form, however symbolic, then reconciliation remains a long way off.

At the end of its full term of life in October 1998, the TRC submitted its final report in five volumes to the parliament. The volumes contain the commission's struggles to understand and carry out its task, its record of many immensely pain-filled accounts of suffering, and its conclusions and recommendations to the country. The TRC was very clear that its work was only one contribution to the long-term work of healing the deep wounds of the country. Whatever criticisms and legal fights the commission had to go through, there is no doubt that they acted with the consent and respect of the nation. In two and a half years they had achieved an extraordinary amount. Desmond Tutu's book, *No Future Without Forgiveness,* gives a detailed and personal account of the life of the commission, and offers his own understanding of the place of forgiveness at personal and political levels.

Working on the commission

I travelled to Cape Town to meet some of those who had worked with the TRC, as well as others who worked with those trying to come to terms with their memories. I could not pretend to understand the situation, and I hardly knew how to ask what they had learned from the process.

Mary Burton: TRC Commissioner

I found it a very difficult experience to serve as one of the seventeen commissioners. It was a duty, but it was also a privilege. I do think it achieved, and is continuing to achieve, through the amnesty process, signal success in the area of truth. Of course, not the whole truth, not the perfect truth, but it brought out things that had been either unknown or denied in a way that makes it impossible to deny them any longer. When we look back, I think we will see that it was responsible for taking the process further than other similar commissions have done. Although individual people may feel dissatisfied with the way their story was told, the country is in a very different place from where it was three years ago.

Charles Villa-Vicencio: Director of Research for the TRC

I come out of this experience more cautious about my use of the word "reconciliation." Some people are able to be reconciled, some people are able to forgive, other people refuse to forgive. And who am I to tell them to forgive? The phrase I found myself gravitating toward, at a political level rather than an individual level, was "peaceful coexistence." That is what we sought to accomplish in this country.

People often forget that ten years ago we were killing one another in the streets of Cape Town. Today we have learned to coexist. We still disagree, we argue, we fight, we scream, but by God's grace we are not killing each other, at least not as systematically as we were in the past, and that's an improvement. Hopefully in the process we'll even learn to respect one another, maybe even trust one another. I see forgiveness and reconciliation as following somewhere down the line.

Everyone was clear that there was no going back, that there had been a fundamental shift in South Africa. The TRC had created a time and space within which the nation could reflect on its past. Stories from all sides could be heard and respected within a safe and secure space. They came from those who had been captured and "turned" and then forced to betray their comrades to death. Some stories came from perpetrators of the violence. But the vast majority came from people who had suffered at the hands of the police and security forces of the apartheid regime. They were seeking recovery of personal dignity and recognition of their family's suffering and loss in their moment of vindication. They were seeking a modicum of truth about the past: What happened? Who did it? Why? Where are the bodies so that we can give them a decent burial and honour our dead?

Ubuntu

The commission carried the general support of the country and a deep respect for what it was trying to do. The fact that it had been set up and funded by the state under the interim constitution was fundamentally important to their work. It said that the nation wanted to hear from all its people on every side of every divide in the country, to hear them with respect and attention with a view to begin healing some of the horrendous divisions. The government itself was trying to discover what it meant for people of different races to co-exist one with another where there had been such enmity before. The TRC had sought to tap into the country's capacity for *ubuntu*, a term from the Nguni languages, called *botho* in the Sotho languages:

> *Ubuntu* is very difficult to render into a Western language. It speaks of the very essence of being human: generous, hospitable, friendly, caring, and compassionate. They share what they have. It also means my humanity is caught up, is inextricably bound up, in theirs. We belong in a bundle of life. We say, "A person is a person through other people." It is not, "I think therefore I am." It says rather: "I am human because I belong." I participate, I share. A person with *ubuntu* is open and available to others, affirming of others, does not feel threatened that others are able and good; for he or she has a proper self-assurance that comes from knowing that he or she belongs to a greater whole and is diminished when others are humiliated or diminished, when others are tortured

or oppressed, or treated as if they were less than who they are.[1]

Ubuntu is an understanding of humanity more at home in Africa than in the individualism of the West. However, Christian belief at one time held similar views, as John Donne's well-known, "No man is an island ..." reminds us. From that basis we can understand why the commission laid such emphasis on restorative justice rather than retributive justice. Retributive justice seeks to impose penalties on the offender, and it is often tainted with the desire for revenge. If South Africa were to go down the path of retribution, even if it were possible to do so through the judiciary, the path would lead to a bloodbath.

Restorative justice seeks to restore both victim and perpetrator to membership in one society. This approach does not minimize the grievous nature of the inhuman acts, but emphasizes accountability rather than punishment, and advocates a prominent role for the survivor in the process. On an individual basis the TRC makes it possible for perpetrators to be re-integrated into their communities at the behest of survivors, provided that the latter feel the perpetrator has taken responsibility for the actions and made some form of restitution. At a national level the TRC offers the possibility of learning from the past while contributing at least to co-existence.[2]

---

1   Desmond Tutu, *No Future Without Forgiveness*, pp. 34ff.
2   Brandon Hamber and Steve Kimber, *From Truth to Transformation* (London: Catholic Institute for International Relations, 1998), p. 11.

Has it happened? In a few rare cases perpetrators have attempted to make direct amends to the victims or survivors. Some forgiveness has taken place, and these occasions have been celebrated as possible models for others. Many have been astonished at the generosity or magnanimity of those who told their story of suffering. The commissioners registered their sadness that this was not matched by a similar generosity of spirit from the white community (which on the whole did not participate in the hearings) nor from many of the perpetrators. The white political leadership of the National Party, having had the courage to begin the whole process in 1990, could not take the final step of taking full responsibility for all that their government had known and authorized in the past. Even among those who said Sorry, there have been comparatively few cases of making restitution or even contributing to a fund for the support of the victims. There is a long way to go.

Looking ahead

I think at the end of the day, a lady who has lost her child, living in some rural part of Eastern Cape, will perhaps look back in five or ten years' time and say this period of transition in South Africa worked or did not work, not on the basis of whether the killer is still in jail or not, but on the basis of whether there is a better quality of life for all. Whether her other kids have got a school, whether there is a chance they will get a job one day, whether she's got a roof over her head, whether she's got water in her tap and sewerage when she goes to the toilet. The next step in restorative justice is reparation — not just direct financial reparation, not just symbolic reparations, but the narrowing of the gap between rich and poor. *(Charles Villa-Vicencio)*

In building a new South Africa, the transfer of economic power is a top priority. At the moment there are too many people asking themselves what all the suffering was for, when things haven't changed economically for them. Of course, change takes time. Many of the old structures are still in place. Many of the people who used to be in the security forces are still in positions of responsibility. The infection of violence remains high. Health needs are enormous, especially with the threat of TB and AIDS. Education needs total restructuring. Under such pressures it is easy to forget just what changes have already happened.

Mary Burton gave me an example:

An African woman, who is now a member of parliament, was having breakfast one morning with her children at the time when the South African rugby team was going to be playing a match somewhere, and her husband and sons were talking about rugby. She said, "I don't know why you care about rugby. It's still an all-white team and nothing has changed." And her son said, "Yes, Ma, but now they are our whites."

South Africa has an amazing history of creative activity that can help build a country that belongs to everyone and not just to a few. But things remain fragile, and who is bearing the cost?

Paying the cost

It could be said that victims who have suffered in the past have suffered again because they are the ones who pay the price of amnesty. For example, in an open hearing of the Truth and Reconciliation Commission, Gillian Slovo faced those who murdered her mother. The perpetrators showed no remorse at all and treated her and her family with disdain. She wrote a piece called "Evil has a Human Face," in which she faces the truth that some people show no remorse for their evil deeds, that human beings are capable of destroying good people without being sorry for it. The experience brought her little comfort. And I would guess there are many more people in South Africa who have had similar experiences. They have to struggle every day to be creative with the deep grief they carry from the past, and with their feelings against those who have done them harm.

So I turned to those who are trying to help people come to terms with their memories and traumas. Donald Skinner has been involved in healing work with survivors, and currently works at the Trauma Centre in Cape Town. Many of the survivors have been prisoners, and some come from families who have lost members through violence. He reflects:

> The essence of a lot of the trauma work is that people get trapped in the experience of their trauma, and when they get trapped it is very difficult for them to look outside of it. For example, the rape of male prisoners is seldom mentioned, though it happened regularly. When people try to tell their story, the role of silence is very important. It is a protection of the persons themselves. To start talking about their pain

again is very painful. It's also protection of people around them. Other people find it very difficult to hear their story and start disintegrating themselves. Then people put things out of their memory and consciousness.

You learn not to trust anyone in prison, and that learned distrust carries on afterwards. It can also be a matter of shame, especially if people have been broken in detention. Sometimes they want to put their old life behind them and get on with things now, without recognizing how much damage they have sustained, but the damage continues to be acted out through substance abuse, through dreams and nightmares, flashbacks, fears, phobias.

Fr. Michael Lapsley set up the Centre for the Healing of Memories. He had been a thorn in the side of the South African government during the apartheid years. While he was in Zimbabwe, he received a letter bomb that destroyed his hands as well as giving him other injuries. The security forces never admitted responsibility. He brings a particular authority to the work, recognizing that all victims of trauma need to come to terms with their injuries, whether or not they can ever come to the point of forgiveness. He told me:

The reality is that some people will go to their graves — many people will — and the damage will still be there. Even if you could say there is healing, the effect of the damage will still remain and be part of the disfigurement. The question is not, Are there wounds? but, Are the wounds still bleeding, or have they stopped bleeding?

I think people can be healed in all kinds of ways. For

some it's the individual therapist. For some it's falling in love with someone who loves them so deeply that they discover both self and self-worth, and that brings its own healing. For others it's a communal thing — the thing that happens in our workshop that wouldn't happen in a one-to-one relationship because it is a collective process — people listening to their own stories within a group. I think that the group has its own power. We all need to be loved, and we all need space. Working with the pain needs wisdom, the ability to listen, hear, support, encourage, love. My view is that the great faith traditions of the world have gold to be mined, and many people can appropriate the gold from their own faith tradition.

Victims carry enormous responsibility, which they haven't wished upon themselves, toward their own community. When it is seen that people who have been horribly damaged are yet able to be healed, those people become role models for the communities. A community full of rage and bitterness can see that there is another and better way to be on the journey toward healing, just in the same way that the moral force of a Mandela or Tutu can encourage a society in shaping a new moral order.

Amy Biehl was a white American exchange student in Cape Town in 1993. One evening she drove a black friend back to the friend's home in Guguletu, near Cape Town. Near a service station a group of young black men who had just come from a political meeting saw them, stopped the car, attacked, and killed Amy. Two men were convicted of the murder, but were later granted amnesty by the TRC. Amy's parents were present at the hearing and did not oppose their application. Instead, they embraced the parents of the two young men and went on to set up a foundation to send students to Cape Town to help in projects such as training centres for young people. In July 1999 they returned to Guguletu for the launch of a youth club started by the men convicted of Amy's death. After the parents had laid flowers at the site where Amy had died, the men told the crowd of young people from Guguletu, "What happened six years ago was driven by anger. We have learned a hard lesson a hard way. Now we are committed to educating the youth about the important things of life."[3]

South Africa has many stories of extraordinary courage and forgiveness, every one of them costly to the people involved. At the TRC hearings themselves, some perpetrators asked for and received forgiveness from those who had been wounded by their deeds. Archbishop Tutu found in these moments the cause of rejoicing and hope. He could see that forgiveness was essential for people and communities to grow through the past. Other commissioners were more cautious, lest they appeared to demand or pressure victims who were nowhere near ready to consider forgiveness. Charles Villa-Vicencio said to me:

There are some wonderful stories of people being reconciled, for which you can only give thanks to God. But you can't expect it, you can't impose it, above all you can't demand it. You have got to hope that it happens. So in the commission we quickly saw that we couldn't reconcile the

---

3   Cf. article in *Cape Argus* newspaper, Capetown, 12 July 1999.

nation. It would have been stupid to think that a commission sitting for two and a half years could reconcile a nation that had been separated for three hundred years. We couldn't impose reconciliation politically. Morally, psychologically, spiritually, it's absurd, irresponsible, and insensitive to demand it of people.

Fr. Michael Lapsley reflects:

One of the things we try to do frequently in our workshops is unpack what we mean by forgiveness. People often hold on to victimhood, including thereby a refusal to forgive, because all they have is their victimhood. Only when people are listened to and their stories acknowledged, reverenced, and recognized, can they begin the journey toward forgiveness. The Greek word for forgiveness is the same word as "untying a knot"; I think it is very evocative in helping us understand what forgiveness can be about. In South Africa frequently there is no one who says, "I did it, I am sorry, I was wrong"; no one who says, "Please, will you forgive me?" What does it mean to forgive someone who doesn't want to be forgiven, who isn't sorry, who is proud of what they have done?

When we talk in a workshop about forgiveness, we tend to break it down into what happens inside a person, what happens in relation to God, and what happens in relation to the other person. The order in which things happen can vary from situation to situation. Forgiveness talked about in glib, easy, and cheap ways, especially to those who have been violated, adds the burden of enormous pressure rather than allowing forgiveness to be part of the process of liberation.

For a perpetrator, the beginning of the journey is owning up and accepting responsibility. It's also accepting culpability, which means the act was morally wrong. Guilt can play a very healthy role, provided it moves onto remorse — sorrow for what I have done — leading to amendment of life. We have often used the image of stealing a bicycle. I say, "I am the one who stole your bicycle. I am very sorry. Will you forgive me? You are a Christian, aren't you? Of course, you will forgive me. But I'll keep the bike." Giving the bike back is actually an important part of the process.

When the survivor or victim comes to the point of choosing to forgive, they are choosing freedom for themselves and for the other person. It may take many years in fact, step by step, repeating it many times. It's helpful when people begin to see what choosing not to forgive is doing to them. Forget about the perpetrator. Let's talk about what this stuff is doing to you. Once someone can see the damage that's being done by not forgiving, they can be given our support to begin the journey toward being free human beings.

When the Truth Commission let people go, as long as their deeds were acknowledged and recognized, there was a generosity of spirit that is more than individual. It recognized that there is a collective side to forgiveness that is the reverse of collective culpability and collective guilt. When I was in hospital in Australia after I had been bombed in Zimbabwe and was going to have a series of operations, they sent a psychologist to see me. She was a young white South African woman. It was a crisis not for me but for her, because she felt responsible for my being bombed.

The collectivity is real. Evil took a structural form in

apartheid. But legitimate leaders put in place the Truth Commission. We collectively wrote into our constitution the option to go not for revenge but for generosity. The Truth Commission gave a space where people could move on their own journey. The grant of amnesty in certain cases didn't even demand remorse, but it did demand a public statement: "I did it, and what I did was morally evil." The moral content is important, even if the person doesn't personally take it on board, because it assumes a societal view that the deed was wrong, what happened was wrong, and it was wrong that people were tortured.

A chapter entitled "We Do Want to Forgive" in Desmond Tutu's book, *No Future Without Forgiveness,* gives some of the harrowing tales told during the hearings. Some victims could, with extraordinary courage and generosity, reach out to forgive their perpetrators. Many more did not know who the perpetrators were, let alone whether they could forgive them. Others, profoundly damaged by brutality and torture in prison, were still struggling to learn how to live with the deep wounds to their persons. Still others, black and white, had been brutalized by what they had to do as members of the police and security forces, and were now trapped by their memories in a living hell.

There are no simple descriptions of people's situations here and no simple ways out. Yet a country so deeply divided, so deeply wounded by its past, is trying to deal with its darkness with courage and creativity. I left the country with a profound sense of privilege at being able to meet people who continue to live with the hope that, out of the nightmare of the past, it is possible, in Desmond Tutu's phrase, to create a rainbow nation.

Community Forgiveness

*Healing among Aboriginal Peoples
in Canada*

Healing among Aboriginal Peoples in Canada[1]

The context

Amidst anger and upheaval, and despite poverty, ill health, family breakdown, and suicide, the Native peoples of Canada are rediscovering the roots of their cultural identity, rebuilding their communities, and seeking redress for the centuries during which the white conquerors of North America have dispossessed and marginalized them. The 1996 report of the Royal Commission on Aboriginal Peoples begins with these words:

> Canada is a test case for the grand notion ... that dissimilar peoples can share lands, resources, power, and dreams while respecting and sustaining their differences.... But there cannot be peace or harmony unless there is justice....

What Aboriginal people need is straightforward, if not simple:

---

1 The introduction and reflections for this section have been written by Greig Dunn.

- control over their lives in place of the well-meaning but ruinous paternalism of past Canadian governments;
- lands, resources, and self-chosen governments with which to reconstruct social, political, and economic order; and
- time, space, and respect from Canada to heal their spirits and revitalize their cultures.[2]

When Europeans and Aboriginal North Americans first made contact, they met on grounds of approximate equality. In fact, in the wars between the French and British in North America, both sides sought allies among the Aboriginal nations. European law and custom gave, to the state that "discovered" new lands, the right to negotiate issues of trade, allegiance, sovereignty, and land sharing. In practice, however, the Europeans simply assumed sovereignty over the Aboriginal inhabitants, with some attempt to justify doing so on the grounds that they were empowered by God to bring "heathen" peoples into the Christian fold.

Following the British conquest of Canada, the Royal Proclamation of 1763 affirmed this practice by asserting that legal title to all land was vested in the crown, but it also established that Aboriginal lands would be surrendered to the crown only after negotiations leading to treaties between the crown and its Aboriginal subjects. This continues to be the legal framework in which Canadian governments operate. Aboriginal peoples

---

2 *People to People, Nation to Nation: Highlights from the Report of the Royal Commission on Aboriginal Peoples,* Ottawa, 1996, p. ix and p. 3.

have never accepted its legitimacy. They claim the rights of sovereign nations in treating with Canadian governments.

As the number of European settlers grew and treaties were signed, Aboriginal peoples, whose ranks were already decimated by European diseases to which they had no immunity, were marginalized in reserves of land so small that their traditional way of life could not sustain them. The colonizing Europeans regarded that way of life as inferior to their own, and assumed that assimilation into the Christian religion and European culture would naturally improve the lot of Aboriginal peoples. The Indian Acts, passed by the parliament of the new Dominion of Canada, made "Indians" into something like wards of the state, lacking any political rights even over their own lives and communities. The acts were based on the assumption that, over time, Aboriginal peoples would simply be assimilated into the dominant culture.

The means of assimilation devised by the government of Canada was compulsory education under white tutelage. Since Aboriginal peoples were a minority scattered throughout the second largest country in the world, residential schools seemed to be the practical solution to providing education to children from small and remote communities. The government would further assist assimilation by removing the children from their parents and community, and immersing them in a European cultural context. Since missionaries had already developed relations with Native peoples and had pioneered Western education among them, the government agreed to fund the schools and leave staffing and instruction to the churches.

The residential schools continued to function until the mid-

1970s. Since then, former students, now adults, have told of the immense damage done in the schools, where they experienced not education but detention. The most spectacular complaints have described sexual abuse, physical abuse, and underfeeding of the children. More fundamentally, the pain caused to both parents and children by enforced separation over years of a child's life has scarred people to the heart of their being. There are no models of parenting for them to use with their own children. Furthermore, the attempt to assimilate the children into Western culture resulted in many despising their own culture, and thus losing their sense of self-worth. It was the general rule that the children were forbidden to speak their own languages in school, even among themselves.

The result of the system is that many people who survived it have become dysfunctional adults, and live with addictions, disease, and despair in the crushing poverty of small communities or in degradation in cities. Only in the last two or three decades have they found the strength to raise their voices to demand restitution. They insist that, to regain their cultural integrity, self-respect, health, and well-being, they must have control over their own lives and development. In other words, they must have self-government. The Royal Commission report makes the issue clear:

Aboriginal nations accept the need for power sharing with Canada. In return, they ask Canadians to accept that Aboriginal self-government is not, and never can be, a "gift" from an "enlightened" Canada. The right is *inherent* in Aboriginal people and their nationhood and was exercised for centuries before the arrival of European explorers and settlers.[3]

Likewise, they must be able to govern their own economic development, and this implies increasing the extent of the land and resources they already control.

Ironically, it is the Indian Act that has given Aboriginal people their strongest recourse because, by recognizing their collective identity, it inadvertently gave grounds for them to assert their identity as a legal right. Thus, they have been making use of the court system to pursue their objectives. Through the courts they have been establishing their right to self-rule, asserting claims to lands that were traditionally theirs and often even guaranteed to them in treaties broken by non-Natives, seeking restitution for harm done, and re-establishing the integrity of their communities and way of life.

But it has been the stories told in the courts about abuse in residential schools that have especially caught the attention of the non-Native majority. So has the fact that Aboriginal claims for compensation for abuse perpetrated in the schools now amount to billions of dollars in suits against both the federal government and the churches. The government and the churches have spent millions to defend themselves in the courts. In the first case settled in the courts, the victim, who had attended an Anglican-run school in Lytton, British Columbia, received a mere $200,000. Facing huge claims, rising court costs, and protracted litigation, both the churches and the government prefer forms of what is known as Alternative Dispute Resolution.

---

3 *People to People*, p. 25

Confronting
the Abuser

Terry Coyote Aleck's Story
British Columbia

Our people were overwhelmed by the residential school system. All of a sudden we just gave up and said, "Well, let's walk this new path for a while and see what it's all about." But walking that path, our people got lost. We lost identity, language, culture, memories, beliefs, even though deep in our minds and hearts we knew they were still there. But we decided to keep up with the Joneses — to get nice cars, for instance, and work, work, work — in other words, to be materialistic like European culture. Now we find that these things are a necessity.

But we are trying to get back in touch with our roots. We've been through torment in our minds, hearts, emotions, and spirits, and that's why we need healing gatherings. We are trying to get in touch with the child within each of us: how I was raised when I was small, what I remember of my grandmother and grandfather. Those things have been sitting dormant inside me for thirty years. The sweat lodges I'm now running help me and other people to heal the abuses we've been through in residential schools. I suffered sexual abuse along with everything else; as a matter of fact, I was one of the key persons to crack open the story. But before that happened, it took a lot of pain, including alcoholism, drug abuse, and getting lost in the world out there. Basically I just went to work, came back home, and went to whatever parties were going. Life didn't have any meaning.

There's a lot of hatred, anger, resentment, and fear remaining. One big fear I have is how much of what happened in the school I can disclose. A lot of the friends I went to school with committed suicide afterward, because they couldn't handle the emotional pain and the sexual abuse and all the other life issues. After the initial disclosure of abuse in the school, mega numbers of people suddenly came forward and told their stories.

It will take two or three generations even to begin to repair the damage. We've lost a lot of Elders who knew the old ways and could have helped us with their teachings. I remember some of them because in the early 1980s I started vidoetaping them at gatherings of Elders. All it takes is someone to prepare food traditionally for them and you could have hours and hours of tapes. I'm very grateful for those teachings because they brought me back home to my roots and gave me something to work with.

For years I've carried hurt from one relationship to another, beginning with not understanding my parents. I was taken away from my parents when I was very small and sent to school. My mum's been sober for fourteen years now, and I've been sober for seven, and we're just starting to get to know each other. I'm thirty-six, and we're finally learning how to communicate. That's a big step. It's what a lot of people here are trying to rediscover. My dad died years ago of alcohol disease, and I was glad to spend a few minutes with him before he died. And I'm glad he told me then to do something good with my life.

I'm trained as a counsellor now, and we're working on a brand-new program to help people who have hit bottom and got stuck there, caught in abuse and not wanting to face reality. I had to hit bottom before I could begin the work myself, so for me the work of helping others to heal is wonderful and powerful. And when I'm doing it, I can see my dad, shining up there and saying, "Good job, Son, good job."

When I finally hit bottom, I was looking down the barrel of a 30-30 rifle, but I didn't want to buy it. I didn't want to die. I wanted to find out the causes of the hurt. I've been in and out of relationships, some of them really abusive both verbally and physically, and I decided that for a while I'd better stay out of relationships until I could understand what was going on inside. It was my dad's words that stuck with me when I was looking down the barrel of that rifle, and they made me think, "This is the easy way out. This is just copping out of life. There's a lot more to life yet."

There were drugs and alcohol in the room that I could have turned to, but for some reason or other I went down on my knees and prayed. I said, "If you really care for me, love me, and want to help me, God" — I used that word at the time — "send somebody here as a helper." Fifteen minutes later the alcohol and drug counsellor arrived. She lived on the reserve, and she happened to have a key for the house I was renting. "What's going on here?" she asked. She looked at the drugs and the alcohol and the rifle. I replied, "You know, I thank you for showing up. You're the answer to my prayer.'"

That was 7 December 1986, the day I turned around. I went through the detoxification program. I had heard about the DTs and never thought it would happen to me, even though

I had been taking alcohol and cocaine and whatever I could get my hands on. Meanwhile the rent wasn't being paid and the bills weren't being paid. But on that turnaround day I decided to get treatment. It took place at the Round Lake Treatment Centre for Native people. We called each other sisters and brothers. A counsellor was encouraging the sisters to beat a bag — a medicine bag, it was called — as a way of dealing with physical and sexual abuse. I watched them reliving their experiences and taking out their rage, anger, fear, doubt, and confusion on that medicine bag.

When the counsellor asked if there was anybody else who needed to beat on the bag, I stood up, grabbed a three-foot plastic pipe, and beat away. All of a sudden, I found the memories of sexual abuse in the residential school coming up, and I wailed as I hit that bag as hard as I could. That fight was the hardest fight I'd ever been in — harder than all the gang fights in Seattle and Vancouver. It hurt, really hurt. The tears came. I broke into a heat rash. Then as I beat on that bag, the name of the abuser came up. That wasn't the only issue. All the memories of neglect by my parents came up. I recalled the way my stepfather had hunted and shot at us with a rifle. Finally my own abusing came up, as I remembered all that I had done to other people, female and even male. I recalled the beatings I had given my brothers and sister. At last I was able to let all this go.

One of the teachings during the six-week program at the treatment centre was that, if you really believe in the healing work, many doors will open for you and many teachers will come to help you. During the rest of my time at the centre I went to sweat lodges, helped around the centre, and opened myself to grow with whatever happened.

After I left I continued working, and finally my counsellor asked if I would like to make a statement about sexual abuse at my school. "Are you serious?" I asked. "Is it necessary?" Her reply startled me: "What if this person is still abusing other children?" But she also said, "We're not going to put another burden on your shoulders; you're already carrying enough." However, by this time I was running sweat lodges to help other people heal besides myself, and as I thought about it, it felt right to make a statement. What if the abuser really was still abusing? I walked around the mountainside, praying for guidance and strength. I called on the water, wind, and trees, and worked on it and prayed about it, and I made a statement to the Royal Canadian Mounted Police.

I talked to them for hours through the tears. I thank the Creator for giving me the strength to take this step forward. As soon as people heard about it, all kinds of people came forward — a lot of other former students spoke up about abuse. The revelations shook me and shocked the whole community. It turned the community upside down as they began to regurgitate two or three generations of abuse.

Oh, it was hard to go back and look at it all again. I continued therapy. I would go down to the river and throw rocks into it, giving each rock the name of a hurt. It was a terrible burden to remember and to tell the story. I had nightmares about it. I've always wondered what I looked like as a kid. My family wasn't one for cameras, but the police found pictures. There were even some of me before I entered residential school. It was good to see those pictures. The police asked if I recognized the other students in the photographs, and all of a sudden their names came rushing back, and it hurt all the more because the children in the pictures were nude. When I look back, I'm glad I took that step forward and all these things happened. The vision is starting to come true — for healing to really begin, it has to start with yourself. For the others who were abused, the healing will have to come from themselves.

When the case came to court, the whole Native community supported us. Lawyers, judges, clerks, and others in the courtroom were crying because the statements were so strong, and my mind curled back to when I was nine years old and the abuse first started. In the courtroom, I cried cleansing tears along with the others until the judge asked if I would like to stop. I said, "No, Your Honour, I need to do this. I need to feel it, and the other people here need to really feel the hurt that was done to myself and many others, including the ones who committed suicide. It's not just to put the whole blame on someone else. It's to say what really happened in your life. Forgiveness isn't there yet. It will come someday, but I know as a help-healer in my community that people have to go through all this first, and say what is true."

I continued, letting the tears flow. And suddenly, the weight wasn't there anymore. Now, after seven years of healing and helping others to heal, I look at how we were assimilated and almost annihilated as a people. But I also see that a few of the Elders were strong enough to retain their values. I was lucky. Before I left, my grandfather took me for a four-day vigil up the mountain in a place where we had to make a trail, and there he passed on to me some of the teachings. But we were torn away from our families, and managed to learn just a little of our language before we were sent to school and had to speak only English, and it frustrates me. When I speak our langugage, the

Elders giggle, and I feel humble and grateful at the same time. But now we're teaching the language to kids in elementary school and high school, and encouraging them to go the Elders and just be.

Now in our community Natives and non-Natives run sweat lodges together and join in talking circles. The non-Native health workers have learned how to use these traditions. It takes a lot of work for us to be able to work together, and a lot of our people find it hard to let go, and to accept, acknowledge, and understand all that has happened to us. Some of us have maybe gone too fast. Healing is life-long. You can't expect people to understand right away when there is so much hatred, anger, fear, frustration, and distrust. Outside facilitators, health workers, doctors, and whoever, could set up thousands of healing programs and nobody would show up for them, because people have already been workshopped to death. They have to take that first tiny step forward by themselves. And we have to continue in our own healing, because there are a lot of issues that haven't been dealt with yet.

When I run a sweat lodge, I run it as if the people were babies that I'm holding in my hands to protect them. That's true also for the non-Natives who join the sweats, including the local bishop and priest. A lot of our people are shy about sharing with non-Natives, and instead of laughing and joking as they do among themselves, they turn all prim and proper. As a helper, I want to be a bridge between the communities. I want to bring non-Native friends into our lodges, our homes, our fishing, our gathering berries. Just being together makes everybody stronger. When I see Native and non-Native children playing together, that's a prayer come true. But it's going to be a long, long struggle to get there, needing enough patience to sit down and watch a blade of grass grow.

All I'm doing is planting seeds. But by doing healing work in my own First Nation, I know I'm fulfilling my purpose, following the instructions my dad gave me to do something good with my life, and doing what the Creator wants us to do.

The Eagle Soaring

Garnet Angeconeb's Story
Ontario

I spent from 1963 till 1969 at a residential school run by the Anglican Church. My parents and my older brother tried to tell me about it, but as a child I couldn't really grasp what they were talking about. I remember them telling me it was this fall I would be going into whatever it was, and there was no choice in the matter. They were as comforting as possible; I'm sure it wasn't easy for them either.

The journey there with my parents was a horrific experience, knowing I was going to have to part from them for a long time. Entering the building was scary, but when it was time to actually say goodbye to my parents, I broke down into crying, wanting to stay with them, wondering why I had to be here and be separated from them and from my home. When I think of it now, I was deprived of the right to a normal family upbringing — the right to have parents to love and enjoy and be nurtured by.

When they left, me parents told me they would come to visit at sixty sleeps from now, and I remember counting off the days on my fingers. On their first visit to my brother and me in the fall of 1963, it wasn't the usual encounter you would expect. We didn't run up and embrace one another. I know my parents were happy to see us, but I broke down and cried, thinking, "Please, Mum and Dad, take me home with you to Lac Seul." I pleaded with them, "Take me with you; I want to be with you." I missed them and I missed the life in the bush — hunting, fishing, trapping, living off the land — all the skills I was just starting to acquire when I had to leave and go to residential school.

I was in a dormitory with forty other boys and a supervisor who had a lot of control over what we did. It was so different from my home, an environment so rigid and regimented. From the time you got up in the morning, you did certain things till breakfast, then it was church, then school, lunch, supper, chores — everything was dictated by the clock. I was scared of some of the supervisors, like my first one. Today I can see that he had respect for me and I had respect for him, but we had to earn respect, and that wasn't easy for kids who had just come in off the trapline. It was a major cultural change.

The principal of the school was an Anglican deacon who was a Native person, and I still have the greatest respect for him, but he also had to follow the policy and guidelines of the church and government that were designed for assimilation to white culture. He had no choice but to work toward taking away our language to assimilate us. We feel the effects of all this today. I think we are a wounded people who are finally starting to deal with the wounds and begin healing.

There is a tremendous feeling of anger inside me, and I know I have to deal with it. About two years ago I confronted and challenged, one on one, the person who sexually abused me in residential school. To prepare myself for that encounter, I had to deal with a wide range of feelings like anger, sadness, bitterness.

There was a strong desire for revenge. I also had feelings of guilt. But I have also felt very happy that I was able to confront this individual, even though there is a continuing and constant denial on his part. It was a very positive feeling to find the strength to confront him and take this thing that had been bottled up inside me all these years, put it on the table, and say, "Here is my challenge. I want to heal and get on with my life."

But three years later, the situation is still unresolved, and I still have many mixed emotions. All this affects relationships with the people I live close to, especially my wife and my children. It's not their fault that I'm going through this. It's good that they should know my past, but it's not easy to tell an eleven- and a thirteen-year-old, "Look, this is what happened in my past." Also, I feel really badly that I haven't been able to discuss it with my parents in any meaningful way. And I've had a difficult time even telling my brother I love him very much; it's not entirely his fault that he leads the life he does because he's carrying very heavy burdens that people hold inside. Many people shut off the past and never deal with wrongdoings.

None of this is easy, but there's hope. On the day I encountered my abuser, I went out to the lake three hours early for the meeting and sat there meditating and praying. By coincidence I happened to run into an old friend who was doing the very same thing. I've been told by our Elders that, whenever you see an eagle flying, that's a sign of good fortune. As I was leaving the school grounds, I looked way up, and there was an eagle soaring in circles, higher and higher. It was a sign of hope.

Taking Back Power

N'kixw'stn James's Story
British Columbia

When I was born, I was given the traditional name N'kixw'stn by the Elders, but when my parents brought me to the church to be baptized, I guess nobody could spell it. The matron, who happened to be with the priest, said, "My name is Ethel, so let's give her the name Ethel."

Then at six I was taken to the residential school. I was excited on my first day of school, but when my mother told the supervisor that my name was N'kixw'stn, she said I had to have an English name. I couldn't understand English, but my mother told me that I had to be called Ethel and respond to that.

I had three strikes against me at that residential school run by non-Natives and the Anglican Church. First, I spoke no English. Second, till I was six years old I was given love and affection from my family and disciplined in the Native way — without abuse. I was a little rascal. Because everybody loved me so much, they would let me do what I wanted. I knew better than to do wrong things, because my family was very spiritual. And third, I took pride in being an Indian. My grandparents told me again and again, "Hold your head up high." When he caught me walking with my head down, my grandfather would hit me on the bottom of my chin, and I would cry because my tongue got hurt.

Being ripped away from my mother was like being ripped out of the womb. They took me and marched me down the hallway. I didn't want to forget my language, and I would speak it to my relations at the school, and I'd get slapped across the mouth or knocked to the floor. They filed us regimentally by size, and I was in the little people's line. I really needed to go to the washroom, but you weren't supposed to step out of line. I put my hand up. A teacher said, "Speak up," but I had been taught by my Elders always to speak gently. So I said, "*Tak may na gan,*" and the teacher slapped me so hard that I fell to the floor and wet myself. Because I had urinated, I got another beating.

I spent twelve years in residential schools, and unlike many others, I never lost my spiritual faith. Because of my parents and grandparents, I maintained my spirituality. And I always tried not to be naughty, because I had been taught that, whatever I did to others, I would receive ten times over myself.

I had been told that if I didn't go to residential school, they would put my mother and father in jail. But when I was seventeen, I took my power back. One day, when I took a crunchy bite out of a crispy apple, a teacher hit me and knocked a piece of apple down my throat. I balled up my fist and gave it to the teacher. They kicked me out of the school for that. I was so happy. I called my mother with the matron and the priest standing right there beside me, and spoke to her in our own language, and in two and a half hours she was there to collect me. I was as excited that day as I was the day I arrived. I finished school in Washington State because my mother really wanted me to earn my diploma.

I used to be on skid row in Vancouver, a chronic alcohol and drug abuser. I went to psychiatrists, but they didn't do anything for me. Then, one time when I was drunk, I called my adopted dad, and he told me to go to sleep right now. Next morning he called and told me to drive home to Lillooet. There the Elders did a sweat lodge ceremony for me, put me on a four-day purification fast, and then did another sweat. The first time I went into the lodge I experienced a lot of emotional upset. Three men were working on me because all my pain came from men. I go to as many sweats as I can, especially when I start yearning for beer, wine, or marijuana.

All my activities on the spiritual path come to me through dreams. I follow my dreams because I'm a dreamer — but not in the Caucasian sense. I dream dreams that come true. I know if earthquakes or volcanoes are going to happen, or if there is going to be a death in the community. My parents and grandparents come to me in dreams, and they always call me N'kixw'stn. So after a year I went to a lawyer's office to change my name officially from Ethel, which only non-Natives call me. It took a while, but there was no legal problem. But then, I had to do a sweat lodge ceremony so that everything that happened to me as Ethel would leave me, and my ancestors would be with me in the lodge and accept me back as N'kixw'stn. Taking back my name means I have taken back my power. I was abused by non-Native society. I was stripped of my language and told I was doing wrong when I was doing Native rituals. I've been called a lazy, dirty, dumb Indian. I'm not going to take it anymore.

I'm going to tell the church to submerge in the water like your Lord Jesus Christ did with me. I want the priest of Lytton to come into the cold water with me and submerge four times. If I can do it, he can do it! As for the church and the clergy, one of the laws laid before us as people of the Creator is that, when we enter another person's environment, we condition our lives to live in it. The church and clergy should enter into our society and become like us. I've travelled all over the world and entered the worlds of black people, yellow people, and many kinds of white people. We're all one family, and we have to respect each other and care for each other. All are brothers and sisters, including the four-legged people and the feathered people. If we all followed the ways of the Creator, there would be harmony and understanding.

I never discriminated against any group — except Caucasians; I couldn't stand them! But now I don't associate them anymore with the people who abused me. Once I had the opportunity to meet two of the teachers from the residential school. In a local store one of them said to me, "Oh, hi, Ethel! How are you?" I said, "As if you give a shit! You weren't concerned before. Why should you care now how I am?" As I was walking out of the store, I ran into her husband, who said, "Oh, hi! It's been a long time. I'm sure glad to see you." I said, "I'm not glad to see you, and I don't know why you're being so nice to me now." I left. And that was the beginning of my healing. I just told them how I felt and left it. I have to pray really hard when I say violent things about the people who abused me, because I know that what I say and wish comes back to me ten times as hard. I'm still working on that.

My belief in the Creator is strong because he has done so much for me in my short lifetime. I know if I continue the path of believing in the Creator and living the way he wants me to, I'll be all right. I'm happy as N'kixw'stn again. Ethel was a dumb, stupid, dirty, ignorant Indian among non-Natives. N'kixw'stn is a proud Indian working for her people. I draw energy from seeing my people happy. I'm going to school again now to be a Native teacher. I'm going to teach my people how to be Native people again. Many Indian children are still experiencing the result of residential schools, but through my teaching there will be healing. True healing is going to take seven generations. My people are on their fourth generation already. It really pleases me, though, when I do an inventory of the band list and see the number of people who are non-alcoholic increasing.

Since the video *The Healing Circle*[1] was made, I've earned my Bachelor's Degree in Education in 1997, and Master's Degree in Adult Education in 2001. I am working in an elementary school where I teach children how to be happy about being Indian, and if they're not Indian, I teach them how to be proud of who they are, and to accept each other.

In 1993 I had a dying experience, and I owe my survival to all the people who prayed for me. A wonderful Anglican priest sat by my bedside for forty days shedding tears and saying many prayers. My survival is proof that prayers are answered for people who pray, and that there is a Creator who blesses us every minute of our lives with special gifts. Let's cherish them.

---

1   Produced by Anglican Video, Anglican Church of Canada, for the Residential Schools Working Group, 1995.

Reflection

What comes next?

At the official level, the churches have made apologies, and both government and churches have gone some distance toward assisting healing in Native communities. There have been official statements on forgiveness from the Native side in return. No one doubts the sincerity of the apologies or the offers of forgiveness, but their meaning in the wider context of an unresolved legacy of domination, injury, and pain is unclear.

Although there are analogies with the situation in South Africa, and some people on both the Native and non-Native side of the divide are aware of the work of the Truth and Reconciliation Commission, the situation in Canada is different, because Native peoples in Canada are a minority of about a million in a population of thirty million. While many non-Natives have some understanding of the problem and genuinely desire just outcomes, many more know little and care little about a problem that is very remote from their lives. Many feel little or no responsibility for problems caused by their predecessors, especially when, from their own perspective, the intentions of those who initiated and pursued the policy of cultural assimilation seemed well-meaning.

The churches have taken the lead in seeking justice and supporting healing initiatives, but some of their members resent the costly court claims against official church bodies, feeling that what was done in the past should not encumber people in the present who had no part in it. Successive governments, both federal and provincial, have sought to avoid confronting Aboriginal issues because so much is involved: not only claims for compensation, but also huge land claims; charges that treaty rights have been abrogated; the festering poverty, violence, and alcohol and drug abuse in Native communities and urban populations. Governments have tended to throw money at problems and tinker with legislation, often with little consultation of Aboriginal people themselves.

Aboriginal people are suspicious of outside offers of help because it feels too much like an updated version of the former colonial control. As Terry Coyote Aleck says, "People have already been workshopped to death." Many are also suspicious of suggestions that methods of Alternative Dispute Resolution would be preferable to the courts, lest this be merely a way out for governments and churches. Nor are they beguiled by offers of reconciliation from a non-Native majority that is likely to lose little by the process, when they themselves are the victims of abuse and an attempt at cultural genocide. Healing, they insist, requires legal and constitutional changes by governments. At the same time, healing must come from within — from within the community and from within individuals.

It is humbling for non-Native Canadians to be welcomed by their Aboriginal brothers and sisters in a way that suggests forgiveness is already taking place. But that experience is reserved only for the relatively few who meet and talk with Aboriginal people about these things. For the majority, forgiveness when it comes may be peculiarly one-sided, with many of those receiving it understanding little of what it is about. One thing is clear: As N'kixw'stn James says, "True healing is going to take seven generations."

Forgiveness in the Christian Gospel

Forgiveness
in the Christian Gospel

Having lived with, and perhaps prayed about, the stories in this book, we can now reflect on Christian faith and the ways that the stories have enriched our understanding of forgiveness. Each of us exchanges stories of our lives from within our own faith, the beliefs by which we interpret life and death, God and what it means to be human. Here, I offer my own heartfelt reflections.

Some time ago I was introduced to icons from the Russian Orthodox tradition, painted with prayer to illuminate some aspect of the Christian faith and to act as a focus for prayer. Andrew Rublev was a master of such painting. Working in the sixteenth century, he produced an icon now called "The Saviour of Zvenigorod," and for me it is one of the most compelling portrayals of Christ that I have ever encountered. Christ seems to be coming around a doorway toward us, looking straight at us with eyes of holiness and compassion. Meditating on this icon, Henri Nouwen commented:

> The one who sees unceasingly the limitless goodness of God came to the world, saw it broken to pieces by human sin and was moved to compassion. The same eyes which see into the heart of God saw the suffering hearts of God's people

and wept. These eyes which burn like fire penetrating God's own interiority, also hold oceans of tears for human sorrow at all times and all places. We see his tender humanity asking us to lay aside our fears and approach him with confidence and love. Seeing Christ leads us to the heart of God which is holy, as well as to the heart of all that is human.[1]

The Christian God is One in Trinity — Father, Son, and Holy Spirit — filled with a dynamic exchange of love, a mutual joy that overflows in energetic creativity and causes this universe to come into being as an object of God's creative delight. God continues to be active in creating and sustaining everything that exists.

I feel it is important to start with the perspective that this universe, this world and all that is in it, is a creation that God loves and continues to engage with now. God regards this earth as a garden of delight, filled with the most incredible variety of creatures and plants in a wonderful, complex balance. God regards each and every person, including the one you meet and yourself, as beloved. The Christian belief that we are made in the image of God means that we have the capacity to relate to God who is beyond our understanding. More than that, we are called to grow into a relationship with God that would take us into an abundance of life we cannot imagine, while God's love draws out our own in response so that we can share in the delight and energy of creation through relationships filled with self-giving love.

To stop there in presenting Christian faith would be to

---

1 Henri Nouwen, *Behold the Beauty of the Lord: Praying with Icons* (Notre Dame, Indiana: Ave Maria Press, 1987), p. 56.

collude with a very individualistic view of human beings. By contrast the African vision of *ubuntu* reminds us that we are interlocked beings, needing each other to learn what the possibilities of loving and being loved might include.

In Christian belief, God calls us to become a people together. In the Old Testament, God called Abraham to be the father of many nations. God called Israel and at Mount Sinai formed them into a people under a covenant with the Lord. In the New Testament, Jesus called a group of disciples to come together and follow him as he laboured to open the hearts of the Jewish people to a deeper vision of what it might mean to be a people in the kingdom of God. The risen Lord returned to his friends, who were meeting in fear behind locked doors, and said to them, "Peace be with you." The Hebrew for peace is *shalom*, meaning, "May all the discordant strands of your hearts and lives be drawn into harmony." While the disciples were filled with joy, Jesus breathed on them and said, '"Receive the Holy Spirit. If you forgive the sins of any, they are forgiven them; if you retain the sins of any they are retained" (John 20:21–23). Jesus was re-creating his community and calling them to become a community of forgiveness through the work of the Spirit within them.

The African proverb, "A person is a person through other people," is true for all of us. We can be tempted to think that what we do doesn't matter very much — our actions might affect one or two others, but on the whole no one else would notice. It is an illusion. If you are working with food that is being sold, then everyone buying that food depends on your standards of hygiene for their continuing health. If you are engineers working on the maintenance of a car or an airplane, then every passenger depends on your standards of care and competence in the way you work. If you are a doctor, then every patient depends on your competence and compassion for their health care. If you are unemployed, your gifts, skills, and possibilities may temporarily be lost to society, but you remain in the web of human relationships. If you are driving a car, then you are trusting other drivers to behave according to the rules of the road, and the engineers to ensure that the road is safe.

Human society can only run on trust. Our life is one deep entanglement of relationships with people — past, present, and future — most of whom we do not know and seldom meet, and within this entanglement what we do, and the values by which we live, matter.

What then is sin?

I began by describing betrayal of trust as sinful. Because human society can only run on trust, then any behaviour by individuals or groups that betrays this trust can be included under the category of sin. In Christian belief, God has entrusted this world to us so that we may become co-creators of life. Anything we do that contributes to the destruction of the earth, its living things, and its people beloved by God betrays the trust God has placed in us. All sin is sin against God. But is there more to sin than betrayal of trust? From the Bible I understand sin in three ways:

- Sin is falling short of returning the unconditional love of God reaching out to us. Our love for each other (and for ourselves) may have marvellous qualities, but it is always conditional to some extent, limited by the measure of self-interest within us. Our love for God and the creation is similarly limited.

- Sin is turning away from God to seek our good solely in created things. Created things are good, but our tendency to exalt them beyond their true worth is idolatry, reflecting a deep alienation and disorientation in our lives and societies. It is worship wrongly directed to things, achievements, status, or people.

- Sin is a proud claim to be self-sufficient in life, claiming a total freedom for ourselves and for the way we live. This claim is an illusion because we are actually fragile creatures who have the gift of life and health for a short time only, and we depend on others every day. Others pay the costs when trust is betrayed by the claim of self-sufficiency.

All the people I spoke to selected stories from their lives that had affected them deeply. Clearly they could have chosen other stories that were less significant to them — a minor cut rather than a deep wound. What impressed me was the messiness, the complexity of the struggle over a long period of time to grow through what they had done or what had been done to them, or both. Sin was revealed in the attitudes and actions that betrayed trust that others had placed in them, or they in others, or they in themselves. Everyone revealed an internal disorder and a struggle to grow within it. Clarity took a long time to emerge. The simple view that forgiveness occurs only when one says, "Sorry," and the other says, "That's okay," is woefully inadequate to what actually happens in people's lives.

Every new sin is like another loss of innocence — another

"fall" — for all the parties involved. For example, two people commit adultery for the first time, and find themselves entrapped in a web of feelings and deceit, adding to the confusion and disorder internally. Repetition adds to the blindness about what is happening. There is a growing disregard for the cost that is being paid, not only by the two, but also by the families, friends, and community. The stories shared here show how sin traps both perpetrator and victim so that they cannot get out. This is true in individual lives and on the larger scale, as in Northern Ireland, South Africa, and Canada.

Hugh Megarry reminds us of personal responsibility. One person pulled the trigger and blinded him, and he had to come to terms with the overturning of his life and with the fact that he may never know who did it. Also, he has had to recognize that he too was part of the problem of divided communities. He must carry personal responsibility for his own attitudes and, in part, for the attitudes of his community, which he had never challenged. In fact, everyone I talked to had to come to terms with what had happened in their lives and take personal responsibility for handling it. In every case there was a struggle to discern the truth of what had happened in the past, and what was happening now. Taking appropriate responsibility is one of the ways we grow through our life experience. Bruce and Amanda show the cost to the victims when perpetrators refuse to acknowledge their responsibility.

Is sin just concerned with actions, morality, and culpability? Both the personal stories and the stories from the communities in Northern Ireland and South Africa indicate otherwise. It is a popular conception that a fully grown person is one who is fundamentally free from outside and internal constraints, one who makes choices on his or her own. This conception is an illusion. Even our freedom to take on personal responsibility is more constrained than we would like to admit.

We are born into a troubled and divided world, into deeply flawed societies and families. We are not in right relations with each other, individually or nationally. We are not in harmony with the earth and are in severe danger of destroying ourselves, along with everything else, by exploiting all things on the earth for our imagined benefit. We are not in right relations with ourselves, our memories, and all that is inside us. We are not in right relationship with God, the source of all that exists, because we live in a culture that for any practical purpose "has no need for God" and privatizes any belief in God: "You can believe if you want to."

Our wills and our lives are deeply infected with this disorder, and it is an illusion to think we can see clearly, let alone make choices from some neutral standpoint. When we try, St. Paul's cry, "the good that I would, I do not; and the evil that I would not, that I do" (Romans 7:19) speaks for our hearts as well. Our portrayal of sin as wilful betrayal of trust is part of a far bigger picture. In this wider view sin is an objective state of affairs, a state of bondage describing our human condition as profoundly disordered. Trapped in a situation far larger than ourselves where sin reigns, we are asked to shape our lives.

Anyone who has experienced the struggle to live with love and integrity in countries dominated by ideologies such as apartheid, or by a communal history of strife as in Northern Ireland, or by attitudes of cultural superiority as in Canada, needs no persuasion about that. But those are only the most obvious examples. Are capitalist democracies free from ideology? Not at all. Just ask those who struggle to protect the environment from exploitation and destruction. Just ask those who are living on the margins in wealthy countries, let alone the vast majority of the Two Thirds World. All of us find ourselves in disordered societies. The disorder is all around us. It is also within us, at the very core of our being. This is not to suggest that we have no personal freedom or responsibility, or that we cannot still glimpse goodness, truth, beauty, and love. But "we see through a glass darkly," and we cannot restore things on our own.

However, if we can see this world as something truly wonderful, pointing beyond itself to the overflowing creative energy of God who brings all things into being and sustains them with delight and love, then we may be able to understand something of the nature of sin. Sin is a turning away from God and the good that comes only from God. The inevitable consequence is grievous damage to a beloved creation. Moreover, for us small and dusty creatures trapped in the world and limited in vision, it is not easy to discern what is sinful. Knowing this, God came to us through his creation in a way we could approach — the birth and ministry of Jesus.

It is wonderful enough that this creation should be an overflow of love. It is mind-boggling that God should love us enough to be willing to come to us through the created means of birth into a human family, as a human being. Being without sin, Jesus was "made" sin, in the sense that he took on our human condition of being separated from God in the disorder of this world, and he allowed himself to be subject to temptation. At the very beginning of Jesus' ministry, the Holy Spirit descended with the words: "Here is my Son, my beloved" (Matthew 3:17; Mark 1:11; Luke 3:22). Such is the overflowing heart of God that he would offer himself in Jesus to bring us love and be vulnerable to human response.

Some were called and stumbled around after him with glimmers of understanding. Others were attracted by his open welcome to all sorts of people. Still others rejected him and, feeling threatened by a teaching and example that challenged their position, developed a hatred that would ultimately lead to his crucifixion. Their response to the presence of the holiness and goodness of God was to kill. On the cross the nature and consequences of sin are clearly seen for what they are — a rejection of the dynamic love of God poured out to create and to heal, a rejection that leads to the destruction of life. It is our human condition, bound in a world of sin, that is taken up on the cross and held in the crucified hands of the One who brought this world into being.

The cross shows us a God taking responsibility for creation and pouring out a costly forgiveness. Evil is absorbed without being returned. Sin is met with a silence that does not condemn us. The resurrection of Christ from the dead declares that no destructive power can overcome the abundant love of God pouring out upon his creation. This costly work of forgiveness continues now, through people, and there are many who would say they could not be a part of such cost without the grace of God working through them.

The cost of forgiveness

Truth

The stories in this collection are about searching for truth: What happened? How did it happen? Who was responsible? Where is the body?

Marian found it took a long time to discover the truth about her sister, let alone face and absorb it. Facing not only the fact of Lucy's death but also the way in which she died was a slow process requiring courage. Marian had to struggle to affirm the worth and beauty of Lucy's life in the face of such a devastating death. Acknowledging the darkness in the world led Marian to face the darkness within herself — the capacity for huge rage and murder that lies in the heart. If she had refused to take that step, the next step would have been to deny her own darkness and project it onto others. The pain would have remained inside and might have led to all sorts of unacknowledged destructive behaviour, such as a life of bitterness or addiction.

Marian recognized the need for grace, knowing that she was not capable of looking at the darkness on her own, let alone trying to shine light into it through ritual, words, and behaviour. In such times we need others we can trust to help us, and we need a faith that helps to make sense of a world in which both goodness and wickedness, both light and dark, have such strength. So Marian struggled with the question, How do we live with the dark without being taken over by the dark?

I was once faced with conducting the funeral of someone I did not know but who, by all accounts, was a hard and sometimes violent man. Both his daughters confirmed this and told me of what they had suffered. In our parish we are encouraged to speak the truth gently rather than pretend, so in the service I was wondering what exactly to say. But first the daughters stood up, and one after the other spoke of their love for their father, which they could never convey to him, and of their hope that one day he would be able to receive it. This was their truth, uttered with compassion and without condemnation. It was a glimpse of the nature of God's judgement.

In my parish, as I try to deal with the consequences of drug-dealing and drug-taking, I have needed to hear comments like this about addiction:

> None of us knows the degree to which other human beings bear responsibility for their behaviour, the degree to which they "could have helped it." That is one important difference between us and God. So even if, for the purposes of discussion, we call an addict's acts immoral acts of sin, we do so provisionally. Perhaps, if we had all the facts, we might downgrade some of these acts to the more general status of moral evils. Indeed, when one observes the rifts and scars of children whose parents took turns slapping, deriding, ignoring, bullying, or, sometimes worse, simply abandoning them; when one observes the wholesale life mismanagement of grownups who have lived for years in the shadow of their bereft childhood, and who attempt with one addictor after another to relieve their distress and to fill those empty places where love should have been settled, only to discover that their addictor keeps enlarging the very void it was meant to fill ... one hesitates to call all this chaos sin.[2]

I would only add that I would indeed call it sin, but in the larger sense of acts emerging from entanglement in a larger

---

2   Cornelius Plantinga, Jr., in Alistair McFadyen and Marcel Sarot, eds., *Forgiveness and Truth: Explorations in Contemporary Theology* (Edinburgh: T&T Clark, 2001), pp. 72ff.

disorder. The warning is clear — Jesus told us not to judge, and the wisdom of that injunction emerges here. We need to exercise the kind of judgement that discerns sin and evil, but condemnation is another matter.

The cry for truth to be told, however provisionally, comes through the stories, whether the private ones or the communal ones in Northern Ireland, South Africa, and Canada. But the stories also show how difficult it is to face the truth. Often it is the embrace of an enfolding, non-judgemental love that allows us to absorb what happened and feel how much pain we have been carrying. There are no "oughts" about the process of coming to terms with the past, and it is very slow. Some find the pain too much to bear; they can neither face it nor let it go, but hold on in a deep paralysis. Dangerous as this position might be, they too need to be respected for coping in the only way they know how. As Amanda knows too well, internal glass walls do not disappear just because we want them to.

Loss and grief

Every funeral after a violent death in Northern Ireland was a time to respect the mystery of the loved one who had been lost, a time to share grief with each other, however helplessly. So many have borne the cost of communal violence — members of each community, the police, soldiers, children, people in the wrong place at the wrong time. Every act of violence was an invasion of people's lives. With each death, after the initial shock had passed, the survivors felt a profound sense of violation, hurt, and loss, giving rise to grief mixed with outrage. What to do? Grief and anger are handled in many different ways, especially when a violent death is involved and people do not know who the killer is. Indeed, the perpetrator may not know who the victim is either.

I spoke to Maura Kiely, a woman who told me of the time her son was shot and killed in a church service in Belfast. After the shock and the denial *("It can't be true, he is going to walk through that door!")* she decided to start a group in which families of all backgrounds who had lost loved ones through the violence could meet and share their stories, grieve in the company of others who understood, and release the feelings of anger, bitterness, fear, and loneliness. The group was tested when families began to come whose members had been in the police or army. People in the group discovered, as have many others, the need to trust each other in order to be honest, to discover the truth of what happened, and to recognize that they would remain fragile. All had suffered, and getting stuck in blaming was not much use. Grieving is a long hard process, Maura told me, and it was so easy to get sucked back into anger or hate. Every day the work began again to remain creative with daily life in ways that were life-giving.

Truth is so important. To "forgive and forget" trivializes the sin and denies the reality that scars hurt long after the event. Forgiveness is not cheap; it does not deny the reality of what happened. "Remember and forgive" is closer to the mark, if by "remembering" we mean not only the hurts but also our need for mercy. Jesus commanded us to "Love your enemies, do good to those who hate you, bless those who curse you, pray for those who abuse you" (Luke 6:27–28), and he bore out the truth of this command in his own life and death.

We need to know that God does love us even when our sin

has alienated us from God. And we need the grace of God enfolding the heart so that we can learn how to forgive. Forgiveness is a way of life that does not deny harsh realities, including anger, but seeks release from the effects of sin. Jesus' command is not directed just to individuals. It challenges the values and spirit of communities and nations as well. Is the identity of a community or nation dependent on anger against enemies, or not?

Shame and guilt

Alongside anger, shame and guilt can emerge as strong forces within people and communities where sin and forgiveness are being addressed. It is not easy to separate shame and guilt, and very often they intertwine.[3] But we retain the instinct that they are not the same, that shame has a very definite meaning of its own. As I understand it, shame arises from a sense of alienation from God, from others, and from ourselves, whereas guilt arises from behaviour that is regarded by society as wrong, a transgression against moral behaviour.

The biblical account of the expulsion of humanity from the Garden of Eden has often been used to exemplify guilt, but it can also be read as an account of the discovery of shame. By eating the forbidden fruit, human beings alienate themselves from the source of life and discover within themselves a knowledge of good and evil. The result is that we cannot discover something that is good without finding a potential for evil. The

---

3   I am indebted to Fraser Watts, "Shame, Sin and Guilt," *Forgiveness and Truth*, chapter 4, as well as to Alistair McFadyen's comments in the introduction, pp. 8–10.

man and the woman find that they are frail, vulnerable, naked, separated, and isolated. And so they hide themselves from God, no longer trusting him completely. Realizing their nakedness and separation from each other, they cover their own genitalia, the means by which new human beings may be created. They have expressed shame.

The story describes our human condition. It is called sin, not in the sense of personal guilt with moral culpability, but in a deeper sense — sin as a state of alienation from the origin of our being in God. When we become conscious of the profound nature of our separation from God, shame manifests itself within us as a deep sense of unworthiness before the holiness of God. In expelling them from the garden, God hides his face from them. This is a mercy, which we all still need. We are not yet ready, we are too fragile, to see God face to face.

Not only are we alienated from God, we are distanced from our true selves. When we deny our inner conscience or our life purpose, for example, we compromise our sense of personal integrity. Eventually, we can become deeply alienated from our essential selves and no longer know who we really are. Sometimes we catch ourselves thinking, saying, or doing things that offend our deepest sense of being human. When we notice and consider these things, they appall us. We feel ashamed of ourselves. We had no idea we were capable of such things.

Sometimes we have internalized standards of behaviour or achievement that have been bred into us or that we have set for ourselves, but we cannot possibly achieve these standards. We may then carry a persistent shame of failure within, because we feel we are always letting ourselves down. Perhaps we need to see ourselves as more fallible, more mixed in motives or capabilities for good and evil, than we want to admit. Humility is not acquired easily, and we are fortunate if we have the persistent, gentle loving of another who says, "I have always known you are like that. That's all right." Learning to love those parts of ourselves of which we are deeply ashamed, learning to forgive ourselves for who we are rather than for something we have done, takes a long time and much patience.

The formation of our personality is deeply affected by the ways we belong to our family and friends and communities. There is the sort of belonging in which each person is respected and each has a part to play in the life of the family or community. Shame then acts positively to signal an alienation that needs to be healed to diminish destructive behaviour and to maintain a healthy social order. Healing circles among Canadian First Nations peoples depend in part on the offender feeling ashamed for having betrayed the group by actions considered unworthy, but at the same time the group provides support and respect for the person who is being made to face his or her own behaviour. The effect is a release for the person, who is more free to be unique and yet belong to the community or family.

Then there is the sort of belonging that gives us a sense of identity within the community, provided we do and believe everything the group demands. Failure to conform may cause shame, but conforming imprisons us within the group's demands, even when those demands deny the worth of our very being. We may be fat and not thin, black or Aboriginal and not white, artistic and not athletic, gay and not straight. We may be told from an early age how useless, how unwanted we are.

Amanda and Jane experienced abuse from an early age, which left a deep scar on their personalities and a profound sense of shame that was carried as a great secret within. Experienced as an accusing sense of worthlessness, the shame was actually a cry of pain, a cry for help. If only another person could be trusted to come near enough to hear the cry and begin the process of healing! Anger can have a positive role here in affirming our own worth and protecting our efforts to develop self-respect, provided we do not betray ourselves by attacking another.

But what happens when conformity leads to activities that are destructive of others? In Belfast, Martie told me that she once heard a man in prison say, "I can't imagine how I did it. I feel I was a different person then. I know it was me, and I'm carrying it, but I now wonder how I ever got to that point." This man had to handle both the guilt for what he had done to others, and the shame of what he was capable of doing to himself by conforming to his community. He was going through something that challenges every person who carries the burden of grievous sin.

It is an incredibly difficult journey. First the man stepped back from all the ways his group used to justify what they did and what he did. That is, he struggled to become his own person, not just an individual whose identity was defined by conforming without question to the values of his group. Because of the acceptance and respect that Martie was able to give this man, without compromising her own integrity, he was beginning to emerge as a unique being. But what sort of belonging would take the place of unquestioning conformity? The man may be asked to recognize that he has participated in a community (Catholic or Protestant) in Northern Ireland whose basic attitudes, defences, and understanding of the past have contributed to the violence there.

Ultimately the challenge will come to the community as well. Will it be able to recognize that its version of history is partial? In the meantime, individuals are struggling with guilt about their own past, and with shame that signals their alienation and questions the nature of their belonging. Can they emerge as individuals within a larger society where both communities have a place in a common history, without denying their origins?

So we can conclude that shame is not the same as guilt. Guilt arises from a sense of wronging others, of betraying trust in personal or societal relationships. As pain is a signal to the body that there is something wrong, so guilt is the pain of moral disorder in the soul.

Guilt occurs when we can recognize that our action or failure to act wounds others — persons, community, environment — and we are at fault. Feeling guilt means surrendering a sense of moral security. We become vulnerable because we have to recognize that we cannot totally control the description of our own past — others see us differently — nor control the effects of our actions and attitudes. Our wrongdoings have consequences far beyond our personal capacity to redress them. Feelings of guilt urge us to seek forgiveness if that is possible, or at least to turn away from the habits of offensive behaviour and make amends if possible.

Can communities and countries take on a collective responsibility for their past? Is there such a thing as communal or national shame and guilt? Leaders in Britain and Ireland make apologies, acknowledging ways that harm has been inflicted in the past, and repudiating past attitudes and behaviour that have been destructive. South Africa set up the Truth and Reconciliation

Commission to try to help all its citizens acknowledge a common history and release some of the immense pain carried by so many in the search for the truth of what had happened. Truth has emerged through the overwhelmingly painful collection of stories from its people, but amnesty is not forgiveness. Canada is just beginning to take its own painful journey to recognize that all its people share in a common history, and that they will require a much deeper acknowledgement of what has happened in that history. Healing of memories may happen at the personal and local level, and that is costly enough. We are at the early stages of working out when and how communities can acknowledge shame and guilt.

Can we say more? The more we have a sense of belonging to a wider humanity, to the environment itself, the more we identify with it. If I visit a very poor country and step outside the tourist zone, I rapidly become aware that the resources I take for granted for my daily living at home are not available for most people in the world. What is worse, these resources come to me at the expense of the poverty of countless others and often at the expense of environmental destruction elsewhere. Our destructive use of power against each other's societies, and against this beautiful earth itself, indicates just how profoundly disordered our lives are.

Our personal choices, values, lifestyles matter. We have more power than we often are willing to recognize. Yet the disorder of humanity is far greater. Isaiah's cry before the holiness of God, "Woe is me! I am lost, for I am a man of unclean lips, and I live among a people of unclean lips; yet my eyes have seen the King, the Lord of hosts!" (Isaiah 6:5) makes much sense. The holy truth of God discerns our true state and condemns sin that is beyond the narrowly personal, but does so within a mercy that seeks our liberation from the bondage of sin. Here shame and guilt are very close. Shame is the pain of the soul that knows itself to be in a state of alienation and cries out for the embracing love that only God can bring through the risen Christ. Guilt is the pain in the soul that seeks to turn us away from our destructive actions and attitudes and toward a love offered to us by Christ through his death and resurrection.

It is even more delicately complicated than that. For I find it has been the Spirit of God working within who gave me the grace and courage to attend to shame by opening my soul to the possibility (dare I trust it?) of being loved unconditionally, and to guilt by daring to receive the forgiveness of others, because I am receiving the forgiveness spoken from the cross. It is a long process, which is encouraged or hindered by the love shared with others, through which God is at work.

Forgiveness and reconciliation

Repentance

There are those who place a strong emphasis on the seriousness of sin and the importance of acknowledging the victim's need for self-respect and justice. They see making things "right" in terms of the law, and justice as providing order for society and punishment of the offender in retribution for the offence. In this model, repentance must come before forgiveness. The offender must be sorry, show remorse and, if possible, make amends; only then might the victim possibly forgive.

Under this approach Jesus' death is understood to satisfy on our behalf the just demands of a holy God angry at our sins. God may well forgive, but the order of justice must be maintained. There are many in the conservative Protestant tradition in Northern Ireland (though not all, by any means) who respond to the violence this way — no forgiveness without repentance. Small wonder they would be outraged at the release of paramilitary prisoners who have shown no repentance.

There is no question about the seriousness of sin, nor of the need for self-respect. But South Africa recognized that to look only for retributive justice was not the way forward out of violence, nor the way in which victims' stories could be adequately heard. To go that route would only have continued the divisions in the society because the search for retributive justice would proceed from rage. Therefore they looked at the possibilities of restorative justice, seeking ways to incorporate all people in their country into one new society.

The Truth and Reconciliation Commission listened to stories, drew out the truth as far as possible, discerned the causes — the corporate as well as personal contributions to the suffering — and challenged every party involved to acknowledge their part in the dreadful history. Archbishop Desmond Tutu, who chaired the TRC, was the only one to use the word "forgiveness" in the commission's final report. It derived from his understanding that the offer of forgiveness comes before repentance because the unconditional love of God comes first. God does not condone the sin but never rejects the sinner. This seems right to me.

Peter tried to repent of his exploitation of the children. He needed a community strong enough to set boundaries within which he could admit his guilt and be encouraged to live a creative life away from children, so that everyone involved could feel safe. The church community in the village tried to provide that. But the village also contained those who did not want restoration, only a retribution that would never be satisfied. The question remains, Can Peter be trusted to live and grow in a context that provides clear boundaries, a level of acceptance, and belonging?

Peace-making in Northern Ireland and South Africa required the state to set parameters within which communities could begin the process of recognizing that everyone's version of events was partial, and that all sides shared a mixture of good and evil in their past. It takes a long time to reach a common understanding of history, and seeking justice by blame, retribution, and litigation does not lead to peace or allow repentance, healing, and forgiveness to develop.

Canadians are just beginning to address their history and recognize the damage done to Aboriginal peoples during the last one hundred and thirty-five years. However, it is difficult for Aboriginal peoples, who are a minority of about a million in a population of over 30 million, to make their voices heard. While many non-Aboriginal Canadians have some understanding of the issues and genuinely desire just outcomes, many more know and care little about a problem remote from their lives.

Those who have stepped forward from the Aboriginal side to accept official apologies and offer forgiveness, and those from the majority who recognize the harm done and support Aboriginal people in their struggle to rebuild their communities and their self-respect, are leading a whole country to a slow awakening. But there is a long way to go before a common history can be acknowledged and the diversity of cultures can be mutually respected and valued. Processes of litigation by themselves do not help each to hear the other, let alone accept responsibility for their part in the past. Forms of Alternative Dispute Resolution, together with legislative reform, may hold the key to the future.

One of the gospel stories that speaks to me comes from Luke 7:36–50. Simon, a Pharisee, invited Jesus and his disciples to a meal. They accepted. It would seem that Jesus was treated with minimum courtesy, but he uttered no complaint, made no demand, stayed at the table. Through a door left open because of the heat, came a woman with a bad name. She saw Jesus reclining on his couch at table and went straight to him, apparently wanting to pour expensive oil on him. We have no reason to suppose she had ever spoken to Jesus, but clearly Jesus' reputation and openness to all sorts of people had given her hope. She came to say thank you with a magnificent gesture, but before she could open the bottle, tears came flooding out. Forgetting herself completely, she did something no decent woman did then in public — she let down her hair to wipe the tears away before carrying on with her gift of oil. Jesus did not say anything to her; he silently accepted the love pouring out from this heartbroken person. But Simon flinched from any possible contact with one called unclean.

Jesus is clear: the love and gratitude, which the woman so courageously pours out, shows that her sins — and Jesus does not deny they were many — have already been forgiven. The offer of forgiveness comes first; it cannot be earned by repentance. Forgiveness is a free and unconditional gift of grace that makes repentance possible. But repentance is necessary to receive the forgiveness and reflect it in our relationships. So Jesus challenged Simon to turn from his own judgemental attitudes and see with gladness the release of another human being from the bondage of sin.

Sin is so serious that God wants us to be freed from its bondage. But the road to such freedom is long and costly, as all the people who shared their stories with me could testify. No one can take that road alone. We need the love of God that Jesus brought through his life, death, and resurrection, when he absorbed all the assaults of sin and evil unto death without ever returning them, so breaking the cycle of sin in which we are all caught. Austin Farrer gave me a picture of repentance that I have always treasured:

> God forgives me with the compassion of his eyes, but my back is turned to him. He takes my head between his hands and turns my face to his to make me smile at him. And though I struggle and hurt those hands — for they are human, though divine, human scarred with nails — though I hurt them, they do not let go until he has smiled me into smiling; and that is the forgiveness of God.[4]

Forgiveness, trust, and reconciliation

We need to keep clear the distinction between forgiveness and reconciliation. Forgiveness may not be offered; it cannot be required. It may be sought through repentance; it cannot be demanded. Those offering forgiveness are vulnerable to indifference from the sinners, and those seeking forgiveness through

---

4   Austin Farrer, *Said or Sung* (London: Faith Press, 1964), p. 59.

repentance are vulnerable to refusal from the victims. Even when both forgiveness and repentance occur, there may not be reconciliation, at least on the human level in this life.

Sin as a betrayal of trust changes everyone involved, and people cannot go back to the way things were before. Nor can communities. If a new relationship and a new community are to emerge, then a bridge of trust needs to be formed anew, and this is not always possible. It may be that one side is dead or unknown or unwilling. It may be that the hurt is so deep that people are unable to trust again. If the desire to forgive the other has to be reaffirmed each day over a long period, the re-growth of trust is even more tender. Reconciliation may be the fulfilment of the process of healing begun through forgiveness, but it may not be completed in this life. Some stories are too appalling, some wounds are too deep for that. But the struggle to forgive and to be forgiven challenges all of us.

Forgiveness as a way of living

Before embarking on the interviews reported in this book, I had not realized just how much is entailed in the struggle to forgive or be forgiven. All the people I met displayed courage in learning how to live with the darkness of sin without and within. "What can give one strength to transcend in some way the reality of human atrocity?" asked Marian. The more courage we have to see with the heart something of the atrocities that we human beings are capable of inflicting on each other, the more we can see the importance of forgiveness as a way of living. Forgiveness lies at the heart of Christian belief. If the cross displays the nature of sin in all its brutality, then the whisper of forgiveness from the cross in the heart of darkness offers hope of redemption.

To wrestle with the darkness, Marian needed to do at least two things. The first was to refuse to remain in victim mode — the passive stance that says, "There is nothing to be done, let us shut away the pain and pretend it isn't there." The second was to recognize her own capacity to inflict harm and her own need to be forgiven and to forgive herself. An important step was to realize that the mess we make in our own lives is precisely the place where God is most creative.

"Mercy and truth are met together, righteousness and peace have kissed each other," says Psalm 85. Both mercy and truth are necessary, and we need help to hold them in balance. There are those who emphasize truth at the cost of mercy. Condemnation rapidly follows, and there is little release into joyous forgiveness. There are others who emphasize mercy at the expense of truth, so trivializing the reality of evil and the wounds inflicted.

Perhaps only in heaven will mercy and truth be met together. In the meantime the struggle continues to be creative with the deep wounds that others have inflicted, or with the history of sin that we ourselves have committed at others' cost, or with a growing appreciation of the bondage we all experience. There has been so much atrocity this past century, that without the quiet struggles of many people to enfold the dark creatively and grow with integrity, there would be little hope for us. There are more candles in the dark than we realise.

Jesus tells Peter that he should forgive seventy times seven. I had always understood those words to mean that we should forgive again when the same person continues to commit an offence. It may be so. But a member of my congregation gave me another insight. Jesus' injunction could also apply to the task of forgiving, or of being forgiven, the one sin day after day for a very long time. We grow into forgiveness and are shaped by it, seeking the place where the heart comes home to rest and forgiveness can be spontaneous and complete with a sense of release and joy. We get glimpses of that place in this life, but we have been cast out of Eden and we are not yet ready for heaven. Even so, there are unexpected moments in this life when the blockage created by sin is shifted, the pain is eased, and we experience the release and healing that the grace of forgiveness brings.

Further Reading

There is a growing number of books on forgiveness. Here are some titles that I have found helpful.

Arnold, Johann Christoph. *The Lost Art of Forgiving: Stories of Healing from the Cancer of Bitterness*. Robertsbridge, Sussex: Plough Publishing House, 1998. A collection of stories showing the healing power of forgiveness.

Coates, Mary Anne. *Sin, Guilt, and Forgiveness*. London: SPCK, 1994. One of a series on pastoral care, looking at the subject from the standpoint of therapy and theology.

Jones, L. Gregory. *Embodying Forgiveness: A Theological Analysis*. Grand Rapids, MI: Eerdmans Publishing Company, 1995. A major theological work and one of the best I have discovered

Llewelyn, Robert. *Memories and Reflections*. London: Darton, Longman & Todd Ltd., 1998. An autobiography including two chapters on Julian of Norwich and her understanding of forgiveness in the Christian faith, arguing strongly that there is no wrath in God.

McFadyen, Alistair. *Bound to Sin: Abuse, Holocaust and the Christian Doctrine of Sin*. Cambridge: Cambridge University Press, 2000. A serious attempt to recover a theological understanding of sin that addresses our contemporary life.

McFadyen, Alistair, and Sarot, Marcel, eds. *Forgiveness and Truth: Explorations in Contemporary Theology*. Edinburgh: T&T Clark, 2001. A rich collection of papers by theologians exploring forgiveness in relation to shame, sin, and guilt. They engage with current situations where forgiveness is urgent but difficult.

Nouwen, Henri J.M. *Behold the Beauty of the Lord: Praying with Icons*. Notre Dame, Indiana: Ave Maria Press, 1987. He meditates on four icons, including *The Saviour of Zvenigorod*, a remarkable picture of Christ looking directly at us.

————— *The Return of the Prodigal Son: A Story of Homecoming*. London: Darton, Longman & Todd Ltd., 1994. A wonderful and deeply personal meditation on the story stimulated by Rembrandt's last picture about the return of the prodigal son.

Townroe, John. "The Practice of Penitence." *Franciscan* 11:1, January 1999. The journal of the Society of Saint Francis (Anglican). This volume also contains articles by Desmond Tutu and Margaret McGrath on the subject of penance and forgiveness.

Williams, Rowan. "Forgiveness." John Todd Memorial Lecture, 1997.

————— *Lost Icons : Reflections on Cultural Bereavement*. Edinburgh: T&T Clark, 2000. Chapter 3 considers remorse in the context of a culture that has lost its way.

————— *Resurrection*. London: Darton, Longman & Todd Ltd., 1982. The best study I know on the subject of resurrection and how forgiveness is an integral part of the Christian understanding of the resurrection of Christ.

Northern Ireland

Faith and Politics Group. *Forgive Us Our Trespasses: Reconciliation and Political Healing in Northern Ireland.* Belfast: Irish School of Ecumenics, 1996. This pamphlet provides clear and substantive direction for communities wanting to undertake political process toward peace, including community leaders, politicians, and the churches.

Falconer, Alan D., and Leichty, Joseph, eds. *Reconciling Memories.* Dublin: Columba Press, 1998. The authors have drawn together papers from several disciplines attempting to analyze and understand the current situation in Ireland and to explore forgiveness as a continuing process.

Frayling, Nicholas. *Pardon and Peace: Making of the Peace Process in Ireland.* London: SPCK, 1996. The fruitful result of time spent listening to many people in both parts of the Ireland.

South Africa

Truth and Reconciliation Commission. *The Truth and Reconciliation Commission of South Africa Report.* London: Macmillan, 1999. Volume 1 introduces the commission's understanding of what it was about and how those working for the commission went about it. Volumes 2 to 4 address gross violations of human rights and the nature of the society in which they occurred. These volumes offer an extraordinary collection of painful stories from many South Africans who wanted their stories to be heard and respected, and who wanted to find out what happened to their loved ones during the apartheid regime 1960 to 1995. Volume 5 offers conclusions reached by the commission.

There is a large and growing literature examining what the TRC did in South Africa. I mention the following, and the first volume provides references to many more.

Burton, Mary. "Looking Back, Moving Forward: Revisiting Conflicts, Striving Toward Peace." A paper given at a conference in Belfast, 9 June 1998, under the auspices of INCORE, based in Belfast. Mary Burton was one of the commissioners of the TRC. This paper gives a description of the work of the TRC and tries to draw out possible future directions for the healing of the country.

Lapsley, Michael. Annual reports from the Institute for Healing of Memories, which he founded in Cape Town after suffering horrific injuries himself resulting from a letter bomb sent to him. Fr. Michael has pioneered his approach to the healing of memories there, and he is well known for his occasional writings and papers on the subject.

Skinner, Donald. *Apartheid's Violent Legacy: A Report on Trauma in the Western Cape*. South Africa: The Trauma Centre for Victims of Violence & Torture, 1998. The report draws on the experience of the trauma centre in working with those suffering from traumatic experiences under apartheid and afterwards, in order to discover appropriate support services for such people.

Slovo, Gillian. *Every Secret Thing: My Family, My Country*. London: Abacus, 1998. Excerpts from this book appeared in *The Guardian Weekend*, 31 October 1998, with the title, "Evil has a human face." The author describes her experience of the public hearings of the TRC, where those who murdered her mother, Ruth First, were applying for amnesty.

Tutu, Desmond. *No Future Without Forgiveness: A Personal Overview of South Africa's Truth and Reconciliation Commission*. London: Rider & Co., 1999. Archbishop Tutu, chairperson of the Truth and Reconciliation Commission, gives his own account of the experience and his deeply spiritual understanding of the process. He was the only person on the commission to use the word "forgiveness" to describe an essential part of the process of healing in South Africa.

Additional Publications

Ignatieff, Michael. *Warrior's Honour: Ethnic War and the Modern Consciousness*. London: Chatto & Windus, 1998. After visiting the war zones of the 1990s where ethnic conflict has become a way of life, the author explores the complex moral dimensions raised by the conflicts, and how they affect all of us.

Riessman, Catherine Kohler. *Narrative Analysis*. London: Sage Publications Ltd., 1993. Here is an academic publication that looks at ways people's histories are heard and analyzed in research.

Path Books

A LIGHT TO MY PATH

We hope that you have enjoyed reading this Path Book. For more information about Path Books, please visit our website at **www.pathbooks.com**. If you have comments or suggestions about Path Books, please write to us at
publisher@pathbooks.com.

Other Path Books

From Fear to Freedom: Abused Wives Find Hope and Healing by Sheila A. Rogers. This book recounts the spiritual journey of five women as they move from childhood into abusive marriages, and then out into self-realization and freedom. The women share their thoughts and feelings about themselves, their abusers, and God. The book offers practical advice for those who have experienced abuse, and for their friends and family.
1-55126-358-0 $19.95

God with Us: The Companionship of Jesus in the Challenges of Life by Herbert O'Driscoll. In thirty-three perceptive meditations, Herbert O'Driscoll considers the challenges of being human, searches key events in the life of Jesus, and discovers new vitality and guidance for our living. He shows us how the healing wisdom and power of Jesus' life can transform our own lives today.
1-55126-359-9 $18.95

The Habit of Hope: In a Changing and Uncertain World by William Hockin. Wise and friendly guidance to help people living in an age of confusion and change to transform personal experience in the light of biblical story.
1-55126-325-4 $14.95

Oceans of Grief and Healing Waters: A Story of Loss and Recovery by Marian Jean Haggerty. With courageous candour and strength, Marian Haggerty tells the story of her journey toward healing from grief, after the death of a loved one. This book can be a wonderful companion for those who are alone and grieving, helping them to understand that they do not journey by themselves.
1-55126-396-3 $16.95

Practical Prayer: Making Space for God in Everyday Life by Anne Tanner. A richly textured presentation of the history, practices, and implications of Christian prayer and meditation to help people live a rewarding life in a stressful world.
1-55126-321-1 $18.95
Meditation CD: 1-55126-348-3 $18.95
Audio cassette: 1-55126-349-1 $16.95
Leader's Guide: 1-55126-347-5 $18.95

Prayer Companion: A Treasury of Personal Meditation by Judith Lawrence. A personal prayer resource providing gems for daily living, meditation, and prayer. A friendly companion to those searching for greater meaning in everyday experience.
1-55126-319-X $18.95

Available from your local bookstore or
Anglican Book Centre, phone 1-800-268-1168
or write 600 Jarvis Street, Toronto, ON M4Y 2J6